....

Shema Yisrael, Adonai Elohaynoo, Adonai Echad.
HEAR, O ISRAEL, THE LORD IS OUR GOD, THE LORD IS ONE

IN THAT DAY

DAVID LEVINE

CREATION HOUSE

IN THAT DAY by David Levine
Published by Creation House
Strang Communications Company
600 Rinehart Road
Lake Mary, Florida 32746
Web site: http://www.creationhouse.com

Photographs © Karen Sandvick. Used by permission.

Unless otherwise noted, all Scripture quotations are from the King James Version of the Bible.

Scripture quotations marked NIV are from the Holy Bible, New International Version. Copyright © 1973, 1978, 1984, International Bible Society. Used by permission.

Scripture quotations marked NAS are from the New American Standard Bible. Copyright © 1960, 1962, 1963, 1968, 1971, 1972, 1973, 1975, 1977 by the Lockman Foundation. Used by permission.

Scripture quotations marked NKJV are from the New King James Version of the Bible. Copyright © 1979, 1980, 1982 by Thomas Nelson Inc., publishers. Used by permission.

Library of Congress Cataloging-in-Publication Data
In that day: Jesus reveals himself to the Jewish people in the last days/ David Levine.
p.   cm.
ISBN: 0-88419-545-7 (paperback)
1. Bible—Prophecies—Jews. 2. Eschatology. 3. Converts from Judaism. 4. Missions to Jews. 5. Judaism (Christian theology)
6. Levine, David, 1954-   I. Title
BS649.J5L42 1998   98-3881
289.9—dc21   CIP

89012345 BBG 87654321
Printed in the United States of America

ACKNOWLEDGMENTS

I WILL FOREVER BE GRATEFUL TO FIVE MEN WHO HAVE POWERFULLY shaped my life. First, I thank my father, Burt Levine, of blessed memory, for having taught me the virtues of justice, truth, kindness, and faithfulness. He also introduced me to good writing. Second, I thank four men who spent themselves to help me grow. Pat Pritchard introduced me to my God, making me jealous for a relationship with the God of my fathers. He taught me the value of personal discipleship, demonstrating through love and service that leadership is relational. John Kepley helped me to see the naturalness of God's supernaturalness, the importance of being led by the Spirit, and the high calling of full-time ministry. David Young taught me that intelligence and the Spirit are comrades; he planted within me a passion for reaching the nations. He gave me opportunity to serve with him and learning experiences that I will treasure for my lifetime. Jonathan Bernis taught me how to understand and articulate the foundations of Messianic Judaism, led me successfully into the Messianic rabbinate, and gave me the opportunity to serve with him in ministering to the Jewish people on an unprecedented scale. He was the first visionary I knew who actually put into practice the things others only dreamed of.

Whatever good you might find in this book is a reflection of some contribution these men have made. Whatever flaws there are in this book are my own.

I also dedicate this book to my wife, Sandy. "Whoso findeth

a wife findeth a good thing, and obtaineth favour of the LORD" (Prov. 18:22). Sandy is my partner in life and ministry, and her love, belief in me, and spiritual depth and insight have made it possible for me to grow and persevere in my calling. Sandy has given me a family to belong to, and she brings joy to me with each day's waking. I am proud that my children, Chris Vaughan and Allison D'Aurizio, can look at her and call her "blessed." Like Ruth, she is causing the house of Israel to increase.

I am also proud to serve with so many fine people who have joined with us for the common cause of Israel's restoration. Stewart and Chantal Winograd, Michael and Kathy Turiano, Boris Grisenko, Alisa Shinova, Mark and Danielle Greenberg, David and Leslye Schneier, Oleg and Lena Scherbakov, Wayne and Bonnie Wilks, Peter and Ginny van der Steur, John and Annette Powledge, Alexandre and Ina Kikinzon, Jim and Ana Copening, Jim and Diane Appel, Jim and Sandra Luciano, Ron and Vinu Goldberg, Alex and Nina Boutakov, Valentin and Tatyana Sviontek, Victor and Raisa Khokhlan, Samuel Cipen, Maris and Iris Salmins, Sergiy Pinchuk, Anton Antonovich, Andre and Alyesa Kmit, and many, many more deserve credit.

Special thanks also to Kellie Rogers, my assistant, who has helped me concentrate on ministry while she attended to so many administrative details.

I bless Jeffrey Levinson for recommending me for this project, and his wife, Rachel, for their friendship and support. Thanks also to Tom Freiling, my publisher, for taking on this project. And I owe a huge debt of gratitude to my editor, Alyse Lounsberry, for shepherding this book from beginning to end. She believed in me and this book, and has cheered me on. Blessings also to Stephen and Joy Strang for making Creation House a reality.

CONTENTS

PROLOGUE

I LEANED AGAINST THE FENCEPOST AND HEARD THESE WORDS COME spilling from my mouth. "So, tell me—what do you believe?"

Sandy and I had married on May 23, 1976, and we had come to pick up a wedding present from Pat and Heather Pritchard. Heather worked at Sandy's plant store, The Gazebo, and she and Pat were Sandy's friends, not mine. Sandy had told me that Pat and Heather were Charismatic Christians, and that had required a bit of explanation, which had left me curious. "Charismatics believed," Sandy said, "that they could do miracles just as Jesus had done."

I was a radio journalist, and a Jew, and this statement piqued my journalistic interest. Now I was at the Pritchards' home, at their garden, in fact, and I wanted to know more.

Pat was a former hippie, a true alternative-culture advocate until he was dramatically transformed by Jesus. Countercultural as he was, Pat spent some time in rural Arkansas, living as a back-to-the-land Christian among the normally staid Arkansas Pentecostals. At one point, Pat had lived in a teepee, which he had built in Heather's backyard. I vaguely remember hearing something about a hard freeze causing the teepee to become brittle and to shatter, ending Pat's glorious native-American period. When I met Pat, he was a carpenter and woodworker, just like the One whom he followed so devotedly. Pat's casual but serious manner appealed to me, and I liked his voice and the way he spoke.

I am not sure what I expected to hear, but I was surprised when Pat began to speak about his faith in the God of Israel. His friendly eyes locked with mine, and he told me about the living God of Abraham, Isaac, and Jacob. God's love for the Jewish people, God's faithfulness to the Jews in the land of Israel, His purposes for the Jewish people were expressed with such sincerity and hope that it startled me.

After some time, I said, "Everything you're saying rings true and is touching my heart. You are really good at this. Most Christians have offended me, but you haven't. You must have talked with a lot of Jews before. How many have you talked with?"

"You're the first," Pat answered.

How could I have known that day that Yeshua's plans for Sandy and me would take us around the world several times over, or that He would use us to reach out to the Jewish people in places like Latvia and Russia, Ukraine, and even Israel? How could I have foreseen that in the years to come, everywhere I went, I would have conversations identical to the one with Pat, in which I would speak of Yeshua with the same openness and naturalness and ease? Because of the Holy Spirit's deep conviction within me, I came to know Yeshua as Messiah as a result of our encounter that day in Pat's garden. Since that day, because of His plan for my life, I have shared Yeshua with my people—a people driven and dispersed, scattered and searching, hungry for God, and always, always hoping. . . .

These are exciting times to be a Jew, these last days, for Scripture states, "In that day . . . the Lord shall set his hand again the second time to recover the remnant of his people . . . and he shall set up an ensign for the nations, and shall assemble the outcasts of Israel, and gather together the dispersed of Judah from the four corners of the earth" (Isa. 11:11–12).

—David Levine
Jacksonville, Florida

הקדמה

INTRODUCTION

· ·

Blessed are You, Lord our God, King of the universe,
who has chosen us from among all the nations and given us His
Torah. Blessed are You, God, giver of the Torah.
—BLESSING RECITED BY ONE
RECEIVING AN *aliyah* TO THE TORAH

EVERY SEVENTH YEAR, THE *TORAH* SAYS, THE LAND OF ISRAEL IS TO take a rest, its own *Shabbat* to the Lord. In exchange, the Lord promises that on each sixth year, the land will yield a triple harvest. While a double harvest would be absolutely necessary in order to sustain the people until the farming resumes, the triple harvest is only necessary once every fifty years.

After seven cycles of these *Shabbats,* the fiftieth year of the cycle marks what the Bible calls the "Jubilee" year. This fiftieth year becomes a second *Shabbat* for the land, and the triple harvest carries the people through the two years of rest.

Today, no one knows for sure when the Jubilee should be, and in fact the land is not given her rest. But with the year 1998 comes the modern state of Israel's fiftieth birthday, and so Jewish leaders and communities all over the world have determined that this will be Israel's Jubilee. Founded in 1948 with a vote and a land allocation from the United Nations, Israel was in battle twenty-five years later in 1973 during the Six Day War, which we now realize marked the midway point to Israel's Jubilee.

The Scripture says that Jubilee is to be proclaimed beginning with *Yom Kippur,* ten days after the start of the Jewish New Year. While in many congregations, *Yom Kippur* is a somber holiday, I was in Kiev and Zhitomir, Ukraine, on

Yom Kippur. In both cities, we rejoiced that God has provided us with a perfect sacrifice for our sin. So now, when we confess our sin, we are certain that He is faithful and just to forgive us our sin, and to cleanse us of all our unrighteousness (1 John 1:9). During the times of ministry in both cities, I was privileged to see many Jewish people, plus non-Jews, come to the Lord. That *Yom Kippur* marked the beginning, in a sense, of a Jubilee period. It was appropriate that this *Yom Kippur* would be a time of joy, not heaviness. Though of course it is a serious matter to confront our sin, God's forgiveness is just as serious. His mercy, we're told, triumphs over justice. (See James 2:13.)

None of us is able to see perfectly what is ahead, and, even with revelation, we must be cautious never to overstate or go beyond the bounds of Scripture. But I do think it is possible, on many occasions, to apprehend what is in God's heart and to allow that understanding to arouse both anticipation and faith.

The Promises of Jubilee

As I began to look at Jubilee and its promises, I was struck by several thoughts.

First, the triple harvest is promised. It actually was to come on the sixth year of every seven-year cycle. As I contemplate this, I realize that God desires to offer His substantial provision even *before* the need is present. This is one of the miracles of God's provision. I have found there is the greatest release of provision when we are walking in faithful obedience to His calling. Call it walking by the Spirit, if you will, though it can take on more normal ethical and moral qualities too. However it might be labeled, I have seen that need alone does not always stir God to move. However, when He shows us His ways and we walk along His path no matter how narrow it might get, we find that the vision He gives us is accompanied by His provision.

Many times we make the mistake of chasing after God's blessings. This really isn't necessary. With obedience and faithfulness, God's blessings chase after us, overtake us, and then surround us. No wonder a triple harvest is promised in advance of the need for those who purpose to give the land of Israel her rest. I wonder if the Arab nations might receive something of this triple blessing also, if they would unite together and give Israel a rest for all of the Jubilee year!

Second is the promise that inhabitants of Israel will be restored to their inheritance and possessions. This promise is founded on the idea that God apportioned the land, giving each tribe its own allocation. All buying and selling of land is preconditioned on this fact, and on every Jubilee the land returns to tribes and families as first allocated. While this was to apply to farm land only, not to the land and houses within walled cities, it suggests to us that God is concerned that we receive our inheritance and that anything lost be returned.

When I became a believer, my parents' first response was to disinherit me. I offered to give back my stock in our family business for the token of one dollar, because my parents were offended by the prospect that I might one day give away my share to a church. I was removed from the board of directors of our family business and set outside of the normal life of my family. This didn't last for too long. We were restored to one another, and I spent many later years working together with my parents at our family radio station. But I still have the feeling that something was taken from me and that the fullness of my inheritance was never mine.

Joseph lost his inheritance too. Sold into slavery by his brothers, imprisoned, enslaved, nevertheless the hand of God moved on his behalf, and Joseph was elevated into the position of prime minister of all Egypt. He too faced some of the issues common to the Jubilee year. Through an interpretation of Pharaoh's dream, Joseph understood that Egypt would have seven years of plenty, followed by seven years of lack. Again, provision came before need. Joseph directed the building of storehouses and kept the seven-year surplus for the second seven years of need. Had the Egyptians simply sold the surplus food during the times of abundance, they would have received very little money, because the supply at that time was greater than the demand. But by holding on to the surplus until the time of need, the price Egypt received was far greater.

Joseph had wealth at his access that was far greater than his lost inheritance. He was the second most powerful man in the region—and, during the famine, perhaps the most important man in all the region because of his control over the storehouses of food. But wealth and abundance didn't satisfy his soul. Certainly he was happier to be wealthy and free than to be poor and in prison. But after we have enough of the riches of this world, we realize that they are not able to substitute for eternal riches. And so, Joseph's soul yearned for more than the restoration of his inheritance and possessions.

This leads to the third theme of Jubilee: *Each man of Israel will be restored to his family.* The debtor who has lost his family inheritance receives it back. The one who sold his land to move away from family is given his place back in the family. But again, there is more to this restoration than can be signified by land and wealth.

Joseph was restored to his family. "I am Joseph, your brother," he spoke secretly to those who had sold him into slavery. *Your brother.* He had been overcome first with grief, then with a joy that could not be confined. "You sold me into slavery, but God turned it for good. What was meant for harm has been used to keep and protect us all," Joseph said. (See Genesis 45:4–7; 50:20.)

He wept upon the shoulders of his brothers, while they contemplated the seriousness of what they had done. How many people have simply become numb and forgetful about the broken relationships in their families? How normal it would have been for these brothers to simply forget Joseph, or at least to remember him only as the brother who was lost. Perhaps they deceived themselves. Family secrets can work this way, inducing an amnesia within many people, shrouding the sin and shame in forgetfulness. Yet God lifted off the veil, and an amazing outpouring of reconciliation enabled Joseph to see everything from God's own perspective, sharing hope and gladness with his brothers. No bitterness, no vengeance, no plotting here—simply the simple yearning of a brother who never forgot his own family, but who had been powerless (or so he thought) all those years to take any step toward reconciliation.

How powerless we each can feel when we have suffered alienation and separation from loved ones. If betrayal is the opposite of faithfulness, how easy it is to understand why we might never return to those who rejected us or despised us.

Joseph was restored, and not him alone. The whole family was restored, and this included their father. Reconciliation, thus, is for entire families, and it reaches backward to an earlier generation and forward to the next. That this story is included in the history of the Jewish people is important, for it teaches us how common the history of family fracture is, and how God is able to heal the divisions, even beyond our most realistic expectations, if not our imaginations.

Joseph was not an Egyptian, nor was Jacob/Israel. Ultimately they belonged in Israel, the land promised to their forefathers. But before they could go up, they would face again another tragedy—the enslavement in Egypt.

How symmetrical our history can be. Joseph was brought out of slavery, hidden away until the time of restoration is full. Moses too—separated from his own people while an infant, raised in Pharaoh's court, driven into the wilderness, away from his family and his adopted family, returned to lead his own people out of slavery. And as he does, he shows himself as Israel's first redeemer and lawgiver, her favorite son.

But Moses himself said there would be one coming like him in the future, and we, the Jewish people, are to listen to Him. No wonder then that Isaiah describes this coming Redeemer as one without fame or regard, without His own beauty or glory. He too would be separated from His people, and they would look upon Him as one despised and rejected; they would regard His tribulation and even His death as God's judgment. Yet the prophet says this is a serious misreading, for His death is for the sins of the people, not His own sin, and He cannot even be held down by His own death.

For so many years the Jewish people waited for the promised Redeemer, Messiah, *Mashiach,* the anointed one, but when He came, He was like Joseph to us. And we set Him outside the family and did our best to forget Him.

A PERIOD OF RESTORATION

I believe that Israel's Jubilee will signal a new period of restoration, each man to his family, and that it has the potential to touch profoundly the Jewish people and Christians worldwide.

There are two ways I believe that this restoration may work.

Yeshua's Restoration to His Own People

This first restoration is most important. For nearly twenty centuries, Jewish people have disregarded Yeshua as if He didn't belong to us. Not only does Yeshua belong to the Jewish people, but the Jewish people belong to Him. If Joseph's heart must have suffered—and his father's surely did—how can it not be true that Yeshua's heart has been broken all these many years? How He must be longing for His own people! Though despised, rejected like *Yom Kippur's* scapegoat, the sins of Israel were piled upon Him, and He was sent far away, forever it would seem, to be distanced from the Jewish people. Yet now in this day, Yeshua returns for His people.

And He comes back with His own passion, compassion, mercy, and love. Like Joseph, He harbors no bitterness. Revenge has no grip on His heart. Like Joseph, He sees the master plan working to preserve the Jewish people, and He sees God's victory swallowing up the now pitiful plans of the enemy. The Lord longs, we are told, to be gracious unto us. He draws near to the contrite and the lowly of heart.

In a moment of tender prayer and meditation, Yeshua's heartbreak became mine for an instant. Oh, His suffering, His unbearably sad circumstance! But in a moment, His hope became mine. The faith of God, God's very own faith, is able to reach into the crevices of our hearts, bringing cleansing to even the darkest sorrows.

Whatever restoration may take place through the season of Jubilee, I hope that it will first take place between Yeshua and His own Jewish people. I look for outward signs of this, and they have already been coming. Many times, grace is like the dawn—a slow, steady process with its own first light; then it comes fully with the new day. I anticipate the dawning of restoration in our lifetimes since first light has clearly come. That's why there are now more Jewish believers today, according to antimissionary reports, than there have been in the last nineteen centuries. It is not that the Jewish people have simply lost their resistance and are now assimilating into a dominant religion; it is that we are losing our spiritual blindness because the veil is being lifted off. The same kind of amnesia is being broken as that which comes off families when they stop keeping dreadful secrets.

Certainly there will be the naysayers who will measure revival one way or another, ultimately to prove that nothing much is happening among the Jewish people. They will, however, be like the hecklers of Nehemiah who wanted only to discourage the work through minimization. Let no man take away from what God Himself is doing for His own sake in restoring the Jewish people.

I yet anticipate that glorious and gripping day that Zechariah foresaw when the Jewish people would look upon Yeshua as one regards an only or firstborn son, recognizing that He was pierced through on our behalf, suffering ignobility and rejection for our sakes. Houses will be filled with Jewish families in mourning, sitting *shiva,* saying the mourner's *Kaddish.* However belated, it will be true mourning, and it will suffice. Huddled in homes, the land will be filled with families, each of whom will lay claim to Yeshua as their own. They will raise an echo, marvelously turned around to the terrible time in Egypt when the plague claimed the life of each firstborn son, and every family wailed in the land. Something like this is coming to Israel and wherever Jews may live, each grieving family a Jewish family this time, each finally coming to grips with the loss of such a dear son. And with that grief will come comfort, as Yeshua promises to draw near to those who honestly and humbly draw near to Him (James 4:8).

Far too many End-Time scenarios and eschatologies have been devised that minimize this coming reconciliation, making the tremendous mistake of disregarding what has already begun in this century, in our lifetimes, and which is increasing speedily. Jewish people are powerfully giving themselves to their Messiah.

When Yeshua came to this earth the first time, He didn't fit into the religious categories and frameworks of the learned and studious. I wouldn't be surprised to see that His Second Coming tears up some of the fine work of our End-Time theologians.

As for me, I want to fix my eyes on Him. I want to see Him ever more clearly, and with my gaze locked on Him, I know that I will be changed. For now, I notice increasingly His Jewishness, and I am not alone. It's as if He is shedding a disguise, or camouflage, or however you might describe whatever has taken place that has allowed people to see Him as anything other than the Jewish Messiah.

In my mind's eye, I see Yeshua dancing the *hora* with His

people as they gather together for praise and worship. I see Him lifting up the cups of wine at the Passover *seder,* breaking *matzah,* washing feet, and showing us what a blessing it is to live together as a redeemed community. I see Him lifting His hands in the manner of the high priest, pronouncing the great blessing of Numbers 6:24–26:

> The LORD bless thee, and keep thee: the LORD make his face shine upon thee, and be gracious unto thee: the LORD lift up his countenance upon thee, and give thee peace.

I see Him laughing and rejoicing with little children, teaching them songs and stories and telling them of the wonders of the patriarchs, prophets, kings, and their lives of faith. I see Him welcoming in the newborn descendants of Abraham, gladly holding the sons in His arms, as they enter through circumcision into Abraham's covenant. I see Him walking to the congregation on *Shabbat,* waiting to be called up to the *bima* to read from the prophets and to work the miracles of Messiah as they promised. I see Him walking among rabbis and priests, heads turning as they say, "He sure looks Jewish!"

Jewish Believers' Restoration to Their Jewishness

There is another aspect to restoration that I know is taking place at this time: Jewish believers are being restored to their own Jewishness. They are gathering increasingly in Messianic Jewish congregations. And, at the same time, they are walking in unity and brotherly love with believers from every nation.

For almost seventeen centuries there has been a spiritual force demanding that Jewish believers abandon their people and identities and take on the identity of the dominant Gentile culture in which they live. Religiously, the Jews were ordered to abandon Jewish lifestyle and practice and to assume a Gentile expression of faith.

But God is using this season of favor to restore the Jewish believer to his own family. It is true that Yeshua does bring division into a household, but it is also true that those who leave mother, father, sister, brother, and houses in this world will receive them back in this world too. The estrangement is not permanent.

> But God does not take away life; instead, he devises ways so that a banished person may not remain estranged from him.
> —2 SAMUEL 14:14, NIV

God's hiding of His face is only for a short while, lest we perish. And this is the day in which He is smiling upon His own, lifting His head up to us, and giving us favor.

While Jews can belong to many different denominations and confessions, something marvelous happens when a visible remnant of Jewish believers assembles in a Messianic congregation. There, Jewish life and identity can be expressed at the congregational level. And there, Jewish life and identity can be nurtured for its expression within families and at the individual level.

How many Jews have had their Jewish appetites awakened when they came to faith? It is far more common that Jewish believers become "better Jews"—that is, more observant by traditional Jewish standards—after they have a revelation of the Jewish Messiah. Frequently, the Messianic Jew is the most observant, knowledgeable, and committed to passing on his Jewish identity to the next generation. While his brothers or sisters may be moving from Conservative Judaism to Reform Judaism, or unaffiliated, the Messianic Jew is finding life in a relationship with the God of Israel and His Son.

I believe that we will see more Messianic congregations and larger congregations too as the impact of Jubilee spreads. I've noticed many Christian pastors with knowledge, love, and commitment regarding the Jewish people and Israel. But it is not uncommon for those pastors to be somewhat alone in their churches. Their members may lack real knowledge and commitment, being left with something more sentimental than love to express to the Jews. I've also seen many Christians humbled by the history of Christian anti-Semitism or complicity during the Holocaust, but so guilt-stricken that they feel they cannot share Yeshua with their Jewish friends.

I believe, though, that we're coming to a turning point where Christian Zionists will be emboldened and equipped to share Yeshua's life and love, not just by a silent witness of compassion or mercy, but by the sharing of God's Word and their own word of testimony. Every Messianic Jew so far has heard the Good News and believed it as a Jew. That's what first makes us who we are. Christians need not be afraid or ashamed of the gospel. Paul said he was "not ashamed of the gospel of Christ: for it is the power of God unto salvation to every one that believeth; to the Jew first, and also to the Greek" (Rom. 1:16).

I too am persuaded, because I have seen so many lives transformed. When we talk about the power of God, I can't help but think of that passage in the *Amidah,* called *Gibor,* where God's power is extolled. In every case, it is His power to heal, restore, renew, and revive—not to destroy. Transformed lives are powerful witnesses. If the Jewish Messiah has changed your life, as He has changed mine, then we have something good to share with others. We must be strong and do it! Yeshua is gathering His people, and we have a share in the work. "In that day there shall be a Root of Jesse, who shall stand as a banner to the people; for the Gentiles shall seek Him, and His resting place shall be glorious. . . . In that day . . . the LORD shall set His hand again the second time to recover the remnant of His people . . ." (Isa. 11:10–11, NKJV). *This is that day.*

ביום ההוא

BaYom HaHoo

···

Shema Yisrael, Adonai Elohaynoo, Adonai Echad,
Hear , O Israel, the Lord is Our God, the Lord is One.
—Deuteronomy 6:4

CHAPTER
ONE

THE AIR WAS CRISP, THE WIND BLOWING, AND THE CROWD STILL outside the concert hall in Kiev had begun to thin out. We had added a matinee to our schedule of festival events because of the overflow the first two nights. So many had come the first two nights that the police had shut down the subway stop nearby so that no more people would come to the hall.

The festival had almost been canceled because of opposition from within the Jewish community. Singlehandedly, the president of the Jewish Council of Ukraine, Ilya Levitas, had intervened with the government against us, and local officials declared that if we couldn't reach an agreement with Levitas we would not be able to have the festivals.

We were able to reach an agreement, coming to terms fairly quickly. We agreed to cancel our saturation-advertising campaign. "It wasn't good for the Jews," Levitas said, "because it made everyone think that Jews have too much money."

We agreed that our festival team wouldn't wear their special T-shirts, which were solid white with printing on the front and looked too much like the uniform of a nationalist fascist group, the White Brotherhood. We agreed to sponsor a full buffet and reception for Holocaust survivors, something we had wanted to do all along.

About one hundred survivors, plus righteous Gentiles

who had rescued Jews, came together for a reception before the first event. And we agreed not to convert anyone to Russian Orthodoxy. This, of course, wasn't a problem for us.

Levitas was rebuked by a key local rabbi for that last term. "They won't convert people to Russian Orthodoxy. They want them to become Messianic Jews," the rabbi excoriated.

Levitas said, "Well, we had to give them *something.*"

ANYA

I had spent so much time in negotiations and preparations and in working hard to get the maximum number of people into the hall. Now I was outside on this Saturday afternoon, and I was approached by a number of people who couldn't get in. In a matter of moments, my perspective had changed from wide-screen to small-screen. Now I was surrounded by a group of individuals, not a mass crowd. And each of these individuals, all shuddering from the cold the same as I, had a story.

The one I remember best came from a woman named Anya, who was wearing a red coat. She wanted to know where God had been on September 29, 1941. That was the day thousands of Jews were first taken to a wooded area called Babi Yar outside Kiev's city center, where the Nazis had set up a mass-execution site.

Anya was the first person I had talked with who had been to Babi Yar. The families of several of my friends had died there, but Anya was the first eyewitness I had met.

Tens of thousands of Jews were executed at Babi Yar. The spot was carefully chosen, in part because it was partially isolated, in part because it made an easy mass grave. Throughout the area were deep ravines. On one side of such a ravine, the Nazis and their collaborators set up machine guns. On the other side, their victims were marched into place. Standing on the edge of the ravine, facing their executioners, the helpless Jews would feel the bullets a moment before they would hear the sounds of machine-gun fire crackling through otherwise total silence.

The guns fired intensely and for so long that some of their barrels melted from the heat. Hour after hour, another line of Jews, and some non-Jews too, were put in place, only to collapse quickly into the mass of dead and dying. Not everyone shot was killed. Many would lie open-eyed, wounded, waiting, wishing to die in this unthinkable echo of Sheol.

But the bodies would continue to fall, one on top of another. Periodically the Nazis would cover the pale bodies with dark soil. Then the ground would move for days, as the near dead struggled alive in their airless graves.

Anya was a little girl that September day in 1941. She and her family were taken to Babi Yar, along with others in their neighborhood. When she was lined up on the edge of the ravine, she was standing next to a Gentile woman whom she knew. Desperate to save this young Jewish girl's life, the woman pushed Anya a split second before the machine-gun bullets arrived. Anya fell into the grave without any bullet wound. Upon her fell the bodies of the woman and members of her family. More bodies fell upon this little child, who lay quietly in shock and trauma. As dusk approached, Anya realized that she must escape. With the cover of darkness, she crawled out from the entanglement of bodies, out from under the scant covering of top soil, and crept through the woods.

She made her way to a Gentile family—how, she is not sure—and they took pity on her, took her in, cleaned the blood and dirt off her, clothed her, and hid her for the remainder of the Nazi occupation.

Anya looked at me, not with hatred, or even bitterness. Her honest question was an expression of her sincere desire to find the promised God of her people. *Where was God on September 29?*

WHERE WAS GOD ON SEPTEMBER 29?

I remember the sense I had, that moment, that God had chosen this time to show Himself to Anya and those in her company. *What can I say,* I thought, *that will help this woman?* I decided I would tell her the simple truth.

"We live in a world touched by evil," I began. I continued, telling her that we all know how evil the world is. Despite all the love, there is something that has gone wrong. God loves the Jewish people, and yet He and the Jewish people have a common enemy.

In our hearts is a yearning for another kind of world—one without evil, without death, without hatred. That yearning has been given to us by God, and it is a desire that we have to live in His presence. We long for the time when there is no longer any sickness or disease, when every tear has been dried, when kindness and love prevail. Because we have this longing, we wait with anticipation for this new day, what we Jews know as *HaOlam Haba,* "the world to come." But in this present world, there is suffering and evil. We know this all too well.

There is a spiritual enemy bent on destroying the Jewish people. God has a plan for the Jewish people, yet the enemy of God opposes His plan and His people. Pharaoh was moved by this spiritual enemy. Haman was moved by him. Hitler was one among many—though the worst—who was animated by that same spiritual wickedness.

But God has promised to preserve a remnant of the Jewish people no matter how great the opposition may be. And He has been faithful to save a remnant. Anya and I, and all the other Jewish people there, were alive at the same precise moment in Kiev because God had fulfilled His promise to save a remnant.

Yeshua told the truth to us all when He said, "In this world you will have trouble. But take heart! I have overcome the world" (John 16:33, NIV). He doesn't lie to us, making promises He can't or won't keep. This world, we certainly know, is filled with troubles. We can be thankful that Yeshua Himself has overcome the world and all of its systems of death.

"We have a faithful, kind God," I assured Anya. "He loves each of us, and He has saved you from your enemy. Where was He on September 29, 1941? He was suffering with you, suffering with His very own people. The same thing had happened to Him. When Yeshua was on this earth, He too was handed over to persecutors. He too was condemned to death, though He was certainly innocent of any crime. His life, precious like all life, was taken. But He laid His life down willingly, becoming a sacrifice for our sins.

"He took upon Himself the full penalty for our sin, transferring to us His holy righteousness. How grateful we are that our God understands our suffering, having experienced it Himself. How grateful we are that our God extends forgiveness to us, so that we too can forgive those who have wronged us."

Anya stopped me. "This is the first time I have heard that God was *for* us. I had thought He had been against us."

I asked Anya if she would like to repent and dedicate her life to Yeshua. This required that she know her own sin and be convinced that Yeshua was the Lord who had been raised from the dead. Together with ten or twelve others standing around with us, Anya prayed with me to accept Yeshua. So did the young girl standing next to her.

RESCUED FROM THE HOLOCAUST

Since then, I have heard this same basic story from several people. The details may change. Different dates, different places. The same murderous plan and the same horrific, yet wonderful, rescue. I shudder to think of a child witnessing not only the death of her mother and father, sisters and brothers, but enduring the unspeakable trauma of lying silent in their presence for hours, waiting for the precise moment to escape.

When I speak in the Messianic congregations of the

former Soviet Union and notice Holocaust survivors in the services, I often tell Anya's story. Hers is so remarkably similar to the survivor in Zhitomir, or Minsk, or Odessa, only because God was moving desperately to snatch lives out of the hands of the enemy.

Hodu l'adonai key tov, key l'olam chasdoh, "O give thanks unto the Lord for he is good: for his mercy endureth for ever," the psalmist wrote (Ps. 107:1). "Let the redeemed of the LORD say so, whom he hath redeemed from the hand of the enemy" (v. 2).

In the United States, the children of Holocaust survivors are some of the most hardened, their spiritual world blackened by the memories of their parents. How unpredictable, then, that it would be Holocaust survivors themselves, in the lands that still contain these mass graves, who are discovering the love of God in Yeshua and living lives of faith and hope.

Joel Marcus's extraordinary contemplation, *Jesus and the Holocaust,* considers the sufferings of both Jesus and the Jews among the Nazis, their parallels and relationship. He provokes us all to avoid minimizing the Jewish suffering, and he lets us feel the raw terror and grief:

> Before a person can be killed, he or she must be turned into an object—stripped of humanity and reconstituted in the tormentor's mind as something filthy, fit only to be gotten out of the way, eradicated, liquidated. This metamorphosis is what Nazi propaganda films accomplished so brilliantly when they juxtaposed photographs of stereotypical Jews with shots of swarming rats and insects. They divested the Jews of their human qualities, symbolically transferring them from the sphere of neighborly concern into the bailiwick of the exterminator. . . . And it is precisely this sort of dehumanization that Jesus experienced on the cross, for our benefit.[1]

When I consider Anya's suffering, the suffering of all those who died, and the suffering of those who somehow survived, I am comforted only by the knowledge that God has chosen such a fate for Himself. "Knowing we would despise Him, and smite Him from this earth . . ." one lyricist wrote. Yet, He came innocently, the author of life, full of life, a victim of injustice and wickedness. Yeshua encourages us to hold on to the hope of that coming age, when wickedness will no more be a force with which to contend.

We are on the cusp of *BaYom HaHoo,* "In That Day" (the Hebrew term for this period of transition between the present world and the world to come).

THE BEGINNING OF THE END

The Jewish prophets wrote about a period of time that signaled the beginning of the end of this present era. *BaYom HaHoo,* "In That Day," they called the time of transition. Following that day would be the Messianic Age, which would conclude with the end of days. After that would be only eternity. Jews speak of *HaOlam Hazeh,* "This Present Age," and *HaOlam Habah,* "The Age to Come." Our history is "This Present Age," and our future is "The Age to Come."

The Enlightenment brought with it a view of progress, an improving future, which would lead to the very best of all human accomplishments and history. This view, embraced by secularists everywhere, also infiltrated Judaism and shaped the character and futurology of Reform Judaism and the thinking of most modern American Jews. The future could be bright, if we sought to make the world better.

Tikkun, "the repairing and mending of the world," became like the social gospel, a religious impulse that would guide people wisely into a better future. Without demeaning the importance of acts of kindness and social improvement, we can recognize that this way of thinking worked to reduce the expectation of a personal Messiah, replacing it with an expectation for a Messianic Age. This positivist attitude hangs correctly on one hinge: the idea that there will be a better time ahead. But like a door with two other hinges that are unattached to any solid frame, this idea is deficient, missing the true hope for Messiah's coming and the need for our own repentance and right relationship to God.

So it is safe to say that most modern Jews no longer look for the coming of the Jewish Messiah. Having waited too long, you could say, the expectation is for an age that has Messianic character, but no Messiah. Despite the World Wars and other ensuing tragedies since the Enlightenment began in Western Europe, there is yet persevering this hope in human progress.

Over against this is the not uncommon apocalyptic view of many American Christians. "Don't be misled," they argue. "The end is coming, and it will be terrible. Thank God all we Christians will be snatched away before any real tribulation comes."

But in the former Soviet Union I have discovered a Christianity that is tempered by the reality of so many years of persecution. Did not Richard Wurmbrand go through tribulation when he was tortured? What about the pastors who were sentenced to bitter years of hard labor in the frozen tundra of Siberia for the crime of proclaiming Jesus the Christ? Was that not tribulation for them? And what about persecuted Christians all over the world—in Sudan where they are being massacred, in China where they are being imprisoned and killed, in Muslim lands where converts are beheaded for their faith? Is that not tribulation for them?

So the idea of escaping the Tribulation doesn't capture the eschatological imagination of these persevering saints. Rather they embrace a radical faith, dependent daily on the graciousness of God, committed to the lordship of Jesus, knowing that safety is found in faithfulness and in the company of the Lord.

So while liberal religions, both Jewish and Christian,

might be looking for a Messianic Age, those who found Jesus in difficult times have looked for Messiah Himself. Because they have found Him now, they know that He will come again, returning just as He promised.

These believers are prepared for peril, though they are hoping and working for the good of their countries. "Hope for the best, but prepare for the worst," my father used to say.

SIGNS OF THE END

When will the end come? Why is it so elusive? What signs should we look for?

I must admit that I spend very little time trying to figure out the end of days, or the end of the age. It is perhaps a matter of calling, not just time or inclination. As well, I am troubled by those who would build themselves up by trying to predict, rather than prophesy.

Here are some things I know deeply in my heart. First, trouble will come again to Zion. As God is pouring favor out on Zion, and as the Jewish people are being prepared for revival and the world for redemption, so too the enemy has been preparing his offense. He will bring difficulty to the Jewish people again, and tragically, for sure, it will come as the nations turn against Israel.

When the Bible talks about *Gentiles,* it is not simply speaking of pagans. In fact, most often the term, both in Greek and Hebrew, really means "ethnic people groups." God is concerned for the nations, for the Gentiles, because He wants to make them His disciples. That's why the psalmist speaks of the nations as being the Lord's inheritance. It is also why Paul writes so profoundly to the Ephesians about being joint heirs with Israel. The inheritance promised to Israel, the Jewish people, will be shared with all those who name the name of God as their Lord, and who proclaim with sincere hearts that Yeshua is Lord, the one risen from the dead.

But just as the nations are called by God, so are they called by the devil. That's why nations go astray. I believe the seventy years of Soviet communism are an example of a nation whose calling went astray. Russia has a calling. In fact, it may well be the the most significant calling of all the Gentile nations. In her God-given glory, she is to manifest righteousness, justice, mercy, and faithfulness. She is called to give leadership to all the nations of the world, and uniquely positioned through the modern Russian *diaspora* to do just that. But she stepped into the counterfeit realm during the Soviet years, usurping God's authority and the boundaries of His call. Her leadership became imperialistic, expansionist, and her governance became coercive. In the period of this new era, perhaps she will find her way, and God can use her. But if she doesn't, then disaster will loom.

For every true calling there is a counterfeit calling, similar in quality, but misguided and rebellious. Instead of servant leadership, Russia and her federate allies could slip into national fascism. Her armies, her corporations, and her government could all meld into one fascist realm, and she could again seek a preeminence outside God's grace and calling. If this happens, then those like Dimitry Vasiliev, the leader of *Pamyat,* with his black, jackbooted Praetorian guard, or Vladimir Zhironovsky, the ultra-right-wing extremist who represents an uncivil wing of the Russian people, will take power, and anti-Semitism will certainly take on a familiar face—that of the Black Hundred—Russian nationalists from an earlier time who sought to purify the Russian people through a purging of Jewish and other ethnic presences.

We're warned in Scripture that the nations, indeed all the nations, will turn against Israel. What this means, none of us can be quite sure. At the least, it seems to mean that the seat of power in every people group will take a stand against the Jewish people in some way. It may be a United Nations' vote, it may be national indifference to Israel's need, or it may be an act of aggression. Whatever the actual case turns out to be, one element we must not forget is that the representatives of our world's governments will act unwisely and unfaithfully.

A Redeemer Will Surely Come

Even in the midst of that tragic misstep, redemption will come. A Redeemer comes during our darkest hours, for that is when we truly need Him. But I don't believe that we will be snatched out of all tribulation. I base my position on three major points.

First, in so many times and places true believers have suffered greatly. The truest one of all died on the cross in agony and abandonment. Did not Yeshua experience deep tribulation? Did He not offer His soul up to death? Let us not demean His death by suggesting that we are His superiors, and that in our wisdom we can avoid what He freely chose.

Second, most of the escapist eschatology is the result of a kind of dualism that reflects a historic impulse of anti-Semitism. Here's how it works: There are two realms—the natural, or physical, world and the realm of the spirit. The Jews are destined for the lower realm, the natural, while the church is chosen for the higher realm, the spiritual. So a raptured church may pose no anguish for an anti-Semite. But for a lover of the Jewish people, the doctrine of the pretribulation rapture is not so universally welcome. Many of us believe that we too will experience a tribulation. Like Edith Stein, who beckoned to her sister, saying, "Come, we go to our people," as this Jewish Catholic nun walked to join the other Jews who were being taken away to slaughter, so will many Messianic Jews and Gentile Christians take their stands with the Jewish people, accompanying them into the next tragedy.

Third, those Christians who simply look to escape the future's difficulties may not know the depth of meaning experienced by those who have courageously faced tribulation, persecution, torture, and death. Consider the power hidden within the text of Philippians 3:8–11:

> Yea doubtless, and I count all things but loss for the
> excellency of the knowledge of Christ Jesus my Lord:
> for whom I have suffered the loss of all things, and do
> count them but dung, that I may win Christ, and be
> found in him, not having mine own righteousness,
> which is of the law, but that which is through the faith
> of Christ, the righteousness which is of God by faith:
> That I may know him, and the power of his resurrec-
> tion, and the fellowship of his sufferings, being made
> conformable unto his death; if by any means I might
> attain unto the resurrection of the dead.

Understand the inevitable coupling of the fellowship of
His sufferings with the apprehension of His resurrection.
Look into the eyes of Richard Wurmbrand, the Jewish
Christian who was tortured by Nazis and Communists both,
and you will behold a man who did not escape tribulation,
but who passed through, coming out of the fire with refine-
ment and purity of love. Meet those Christians who endured
the Gulag and its forced labor and deprivations, and you
will see many saintly Russians who count it a prize to have
suffered for the Lord.

At this time, none of us know when Yeshua will return.
Nor can we be certain about all the circumstances that will
surround His coming. The prophecies in Zechariah present
a jumbled chronology and most attempts to simplify them
are motivated by a desire to make everything fit into our
neatly worked eschatology.

The Book of Zechariah speaks of the Lord's returning to
Israel, with all Israel looking upon Him as one whom they
had pierced and mourning for Him as one mourns for an
only son. Then it speaks of tribulation. Then it speaks of a
redemptive act of rescue. Then it speaks of a third of Israel
dying in war. Then it speaks of the nations coming to
Jerusalem to worship the Lord at the festival of *Sukkot,* or

Tabernacles. This is not the typical chronology of many eschatologies taught in the American church today. I won't attempt to overdefine it, but I want to make some important generalizations.

A Time of Trouble

First, Zechariah gives us an important glimpse into the end and shows us that Yeshua chooses to be present with His Jewish people during their troubles. This is significant, because it is consistent with the entire incarnational message of the gospel: that God came as a man to be present with His people, experiencing manhood in fullness, and bringing the godhead in fullness to mankind. As Emmanuel, "God with us," we discover our Father and Lord, who rescues us from death's dominion and transfers us into the kingdom of His dearly loved Son. This God who is present with His people is capable of announcing good news to the captives, prisoners, poor, and diseased. Every aspect of Yeshua's coming, including His return, is still good news. Just as Yeshua rose from His grave in Jerusalem to be among the Jewish people, so Yeshua comes down to earth yet again to be among His Jewish people. This is the Lord, manifesting infinite love and personal faithfulness to a thousand generations.

Second, Zechariah shows us that a veil will be lifted off Jewish eyes, and they will behold Yeshua and recognize Him fully and finally. But this moment is not an excuse to postpone Jewish-directed evangelism. It is a reprise of every moment when Yeshua is welcomed into the heart of a Jewish person. We *all* have gone astray, and the Lord has laid upon Yeshua *the iniquity of us all* (Isa. 53:6). He has become our sacrifice. When we finally see this, it is impossible not to grieve. Let no one, in the name of eschatology, abandon Yeshua's personal commitment to bring the good news now to every generation. Let no one, in the name of an End-Time Jewish revival, postpone Jewish-directed evangelism until some post-tribulational period. *Now* is the time to favor Zion, and blessed are those who bless Abraham. No greater favor can be given to the Jewish people, no greater blessing, than to hear and hearken to the good news of Yeshua, the Messiah.

Third, Zechariah shows that there yet remains tragedy for the Jewish people. None of us may be fatalistic about this, nor can we distance ourselves emotionally as if it is simply a judgment against the Jews. That didn't work in World War II, and it won't work any time in the future. God protect us from those who might rush headlong into an Armageddon scenario, justifying themselves with some misguided sense of the inevitable and the prophetic! We are not able to hurry Yeshua's return; we are only able to anticipate it and welcome it. It is in the hidden counsel of the Father to determine when and how He comes back.

Fourth, Zechariah describes an element of the End Times that has eluded some Christians. Jewish eschatology sees two distinct periods—*this world,* and *the world to come.* They are separated by *that day,* and *the Messianic Age. This world* is the present age with which we are all familiar. *The world to come* is the eternal realm. In between, we have *that day,* which marks a period of transformation. It includes both the terrible and the wonderful. Light and darkness are both increasing, and though it might seem in *that day* that darkness will prevail, *light* in fact is the victor.

THY KINGDOM COME

Zechariah talks about *that day:* "The LORD shall be king over all the earth: in that day shall there be one LORD, and his name one" (Zech. 14:9). That terrible, dark period is contrasted with the wonderful period that marks the full coming of God's kingdom. At the very point that God's rule is inaugurated in a new way on the earth, so is there much opposition. This is why, I believe, the awful extermination of two-thirds of the people takes place as the nations oppose Jerusalem. But the kingdom of God cannot be turned away, and in *that day* it more fully comes. God's rule prevails, and this is the beginning of the end of *this world.*

Yet in the period that we, as Christians, might call the *millennium,* or, as Jews, *the Messianic Age,* King Messiah is ruling, but the nations have not fully determined how they will relate to God on this earth. The nations, according to Zechariah, are commanded to join the Jewish people in celebration in Jerusalem, coming up to the holy city for *Sukkoth,* the holiday of the ingathering. And those nations that refuse, we're told, will face drought and tragedy.

The Book of Revelation echoes this thought, telling us that Yeshua is present on the earth in a glorious Jerusalem. A river proceeds from His throne, and on its banks are planted twelve trees, which are collectively known as the Tree of Life. Bearing fruit in every season, its leaves are for the healing of the nations.

It's not insignificant to note the similarity to Zechariah's vision and John's Revelation. Both see Yeshua on the throne, in Jerusalem, and both see the nations still in need of something more from God. Zechariah pictures the nations as still being autonomous and having to determine if they will join Israel in worshiping God, even in a "Jewish" way. John pictures the nations as still being in need of healing. Perhaps they speak about the same thing.

I personally believe that the nations will be healed as they begin to bless the Jewish people. While the nations are not called to convert to Judaism, or to embrace fully a Jewish manner of worship, there is no doubt that the nations will be asked in the future to join in some of the Jewish celebrations. No wonder, then, that many churches today are seeing this and are gladly "rehearsing" the glorious future by incorporating the biblical feasts into their corporate lives and worship cycle.

Those that refuse, at least in the end, will face some chastisement. Certainly by then, God will demand of the nations that they put off their enmity towards the Jews and be joint heirs with Israel.

Israel Restored

Sometime during this period around *that day* and *the Messianic Age,* Israel will be restored to her full boundaries. Ezekiel speaks of this restoration, telling us that the Jewish people will be returned to their ancestral allotments. Interestingly, the *Gerim,* or Sojourners, will also receive an inheritance. The *Gerim* are Gentiles who have chosen to identify with Jewish people without converting to Judaism. They are recognizable within Israel as non-Jews, but from outside they appear to be Jews. Somehow they are identifiable and distinct. Those who have children and who have taken the bold (some would have said foolish) stand of living with the Jewish people in their land will receive an inheritance of the land. So in this way, the *Gerim* will receive an allotment of land in the land of Israel. This is a provocative concept, rich with meaning, and suggestive of something normally locked up in the term *joint-heir.* Jewish people will have to share their land with non-Jews. We can rehearse this in the present, both by honoring the non-Jews who are called to the Messianic movement and by accepting them into our midst with full honor and privileges.

Some type of history then continues until the ultimate dissolution of death and the final judgment of the adversary of God. This marks the conclusion of the Messianic Age, and the final chapter of all that we know as the temporal world. We will be ushered then into the realm of the eternal, where worship never ceases, where every tear is dried, and where the glory of God fills the whole earth, even the New Earth.

החולמים

THOSE WHO DREAM

....

The Jews who will it shall achieve their state.
— PUBLISHED IN THEODOR HERZL'S WORK, *THE JEWISH STATE* (1896),
LATER KNOWN AS THE MANIFESTO OF THE ZIONIST MOVEMENT

CHAPTER
TWO

SOMETIME IN THE LAST CENTURY, HEAVEN CALLED OUT TO EARTH that the time had come. The bitterness of the affliction, the wanderings, the homelessness, and heartache of being strangers in foreign lands had turned into cries from earth to heaven. And heaven heard. And the Jewish people began to dream dreams and see visions.

> *When the Lord brought back the captives to Zion, we were like men who dreamed.*
> —PSALM 126:1, NIV

Budapest-born journalist, Theodor Herzl, had a vision of the Jewish people in their own land, so, in 1897, he convened the First Zionist Congress in Basel, Switzerland, and the vision spread. Russian-born Eliezer Ben-Yehuda dreamed of a revival of Hebrew as the living language of the Jewish people. So he moved his family to the land, speaking to them only in the sacred tongue of Jewish prayer and study; he single-handedly initiated the revival of everyday Hebrew, a language out of use for centuries. Barely twenty years old, Polish-born David Green dreamed of a free Jewish people in their own land. So he moved to Palestine, became a leader among the young Zionists, and changed his name to David Ben-Gurion. Thirty-two years later, in 1948, he presided over Israel's internationally declared and recognized independence as her first prime minister.

These dreams and visions had one thing in common: They spoke to secret places of the soul, and they contagiously spread like wildfire throughout the hearts, souls, and minds of the Jewish people all over the earth.

Dreams and visions are the language of the Spirit, which reaches into places in our souls that can be touched no other way. They touch believer and nonbeliever alike, Abimelechs and Abrahams, Pharaohs and Josephs, Nebuchadnezzars and Daniels. When there is no evidence, when no man can persuade us, there yet remains a place within us that can hear and understand, see and perceive. That place is somehow open to God's Spirit, able to be stirred and motivated in extraordinary ways.

This part of us is often awakened only when we are asleep. It is the part of us that is alive to symbols, to future realities, to the unknown, and unknowable. And it is a part of us that heaven can reach when nothing else in us will listen.

"Call to me and I will answer you," the Lord promised to Jeremiah, "and tell you great and unsearchable things you do not know" (Jer. 33:3, NIV). There are many things we don't know, and yet we must *come* to know them. The most challenging are those things that are also unsearchable. Despite our best efforts, and the efforts of all whom we know, we will never make the discovery for ourselves. Yet the Lord says He can reveal to us, even show us, that which we can't search out. Life indeed is hidden . . . hidden in Him.

DREAMS AND THE BIRTH OF YESHUA

When Jesus' mother was pregnant out of wedlock, her fiancé, Joseph, considered a quiet end to their engagement. In his day, this required a divorce because betrothal was binding under Jewish law. Joseph could not simply change his mind and ask for an engagement ring back. He had to appeal to a court of Jewish law, whose judges were experts in the *Torah* and its daily application. He could do this privately and quietly, which would be an honorable way to protect Mary from the humiliation of a public divorce. How Joseph's heart must have been troubled by the prospect that his betrothed had been unfaithful even before their wedding night.

In a dream, the Lord Himself spoke to Joseph, advising him not to divorce Mary, but to continue with his plans for marriage. The Lord told Joseph that this child within Mary was not a *mumzer,* illegitimate child, but came from the Holy Spirit. Who could explain or fully understand such an unprecedented thing? No wonder the message came to Joseph in a dream.

Mary and Joseph's son now born, Magi came from the Far East, driven by the portent of a star, seeking in their ominous pursuit of a king, for the fulfillment of an ancient Jewish prophecy. They met with King Herod, and they indeed stirred his fear. A promised king was no doubt a threat to Herod, so he ordered the deaths of all boys in Bethlehem two years old and younger, the city in which this promised king had been prophesied to be born. Often things spoken through dreams and visions are like childbirth itself—accompanied by much suffering. These matters of the Spirit are escorted in with the pain, even the intense agony of labor.

Who can discern between the warnings of the Spirit and the simple temptations of fear? And who can know the unknowable dangers facing us? When God is preparing for redemption, it is as if the rumor of deliverance proceeds even to the gates of hell. Murderous intentions rose up in Herod's heart, and he issued a reprise of Pharaoh's edict generations earlier when he called for the deaths of Jewish babies two years and younger. Still, Moses was spared and set adrift amid the reeds.

When Joseph and Mary needed to gather their belongings and flee for Jesus' life to Egypt to escape Herod, it was through a dream that Joseph understood what must be done. The revelations of God do not go unopposed, and so it is even for children with profound destinies and callings. That same child who is known by God even while he is being knit together in his mother's womb may face an out-pouring of unholy wrath from an enemy hellbent on resisting God's holy plans.

Dreams and visions may open the way for God's working, but they do not bring a guarantee of ease and comfort. Even visitations by God may be discomforting. No wonder then that while God was stirring the hearts and souls of the early Zionists at the opening of the twentieth century, the adversary of God was also being agitated. *Pogroms,* riots against Jews, increased in number and frequency in Russia and the neighboring countries. Jewish boys were conscripted into the tsar's army to be sent to the frontlines as cannon fodder. Forced baptisms led to the state-enforced stealing away of Jewish infants from their families. Indeed, the enmity between the Jew and the Gentile seemed to be increasing, from Germany to Eastern Europe into Russia, at the same time that God was pronouncing favor to Zion.

The patriarchs dreamed. Jacob had a dream of angels ascending and descending from heaven to earth. And Jacob wrestled with God, forever walking with a blessing and a limp as souvenirs. God and heaven on earth, the subjects of Jacob's dream and his dream-like encounter. With this revelation planted in him, Jacob's nature was changed, and so was his name. He was now *Israel,* the "God-wrestler." And the sons of Israel would wrestle with God, if not with each other. And continue to dream dreams.

The Dreamer

Joseph enjoyed the special love and attention of his father, Jacob. And he dreamed about his brothers bowing down to him. Instead, they rose up, threw Joseph into a pit, sold him into slavery, abandoned him, and rejected him. Then they lied to Jacob, saying that he had been killed by a wild animal. It's the kind of reaction that would make you never want to have another dream. But God continued to use dreams in Joseph's life, eventually freeing him from slavery and promoting him to become Egypt's prime minister. Joseph's interpretation of Pharaoh's dream became the basis of the Egyptian plan for harvesting and storing in seven years of plenty in preparation for seven future years of lack.

Again the unsearchable had been revealed through dreams and visions. No one could accurately predict such agricultural abundance or insufficiency. But the Spirit of God spoke through a dream and gave understanding without evidence. And everything came to pass. After the seven years of plenty, a famine did strike the region, affecting not only Egypt but nations up the Mediterranean coast and across the Jordan valley.

The God-wrestler, Jacob, and his sons, feeling the pangs of hunger, ended up in Egypt—the only source for food in the vicinity. In this desperate season, they began to remember the lost son, Joseph. Secretly sold by his brothers into slavery, long thought dead by his father, Joseph had been providentially placed in Egypt to provide a means of safe-keeping for the people of Israel.

The once-rejected Joseph understood that God's hand was always moving, even when it was unseen, and that God's plans to preserve him and the people of Israel could not be overturned by jealousy, famine, sibling rivalry, or satanic interventions.

Just as God worked to move the tribes of Israel to Egypt to be preserved during famine, He also worked to move Jesus and His parents to Egypt to preserve them from the enemy's plans. And when it was time to return to the land of Israel, God again spoke to Joseph in a dream.

A GOD REVEALED

Historically, God has spoken to the Jewish people through dreams and visions. He reveals Himself supernaturally in many other ways. He is committed to revealing Himself so that all will know Him. Whether it is through an angel, a burning bush, or even a talking donkey, God will let His will be known so that people will know how to live their lives. And He'll reveal Himself so that people can have a relationship with Him and be transformed to walk faithfully with Him.

God works through dreams and visions. He directs in this way. He calls things that are not as though they were, bringing reality, if you will, into existence. (See 1 Corinthians 1:28.) *He speaks, and things become real.*

Sometimes He speaks with a voice from heaven so that those who hear will know that they have had a personal encounter with the one true God. I heard a voice from heaven in 1976, and it changed my life. I'll tell you that story soon. But first, I want you to know that the same God who called Abraham, Isaac, Jacob, Moses, the prophet Samuel, King David, and Jeremiah is still calling His Jewish people supernaturally. As He once did during the times of the patriarchs and the kingdoms of Judah and Israel, He also called His people during the times of the apostles. And He is again calling His people by name.

On *Shavuot*, Pentecost in Jerusalem, almost two thousand years ago, one hundred twenty disciples of Jesus began to speak in unknown tongues. *Shavuot* was one of the three Jewish pilgrimage festivals, and Jews from throughout the world were gathered in Jerusalem to celebrate the holiday of firstfruits and the early harvest. These first tongue-speaking disciples drew a lot of attention, and some *Shavuot* celebrants thought for sure they were drunk. However, when Peter explained what was happening—that the Spirit of God was being poured out as the prophet Joel had promised—the people began to marvel. And if these signs were taking place, that meant that dreams and visions would be coming too.

Peter later had a vision of unclean animals descending from heaven in a sheet (Acts 10:11–12). When the Lord told him to eat of these unclean beings, Peter responded that it was impossible because he kept *kosher.* Having aroused such a strong reaction in Peter about things clean and unclean, the Lord then gave a dream to an unclean Gentile in Caesarea. In this dream, the Gentile, Cornelius, called to Peter from Joppa. Cornelius later sent for Peter to find out how to be saved, confirming the dream's prophetic significance in the realm of the natural.

While Peter was delivering his first sermon to Gentiles, the Lord interrupted his message by pouring the Holy Spirit out onto the unclean Gentiles. They also began to speak in unknown tongues, and suddenly Peter understood his own dream about the unclean animals. The Lord later explained to Peter that the dream was about people, not food. Peter realized that God wanted to show His favor to people from every ethnic background, not just Jews.

It was through a supernatural vision that God reached Peter's secret thoughts and prepared him for God's new initiative with the Gentiles. So Peter was ready to receive non-Jews into this growing Messianic Jewish movement in Israel. Even though Peter was called to be an apostle to the Jews, he was used by God to give the official Messianic welcome to the Gentiles who wanted to be saved.

The orthodox Jewish rabbi Shaul—Paul—was riding to Syria in the hope of capturing more Jewish followers of Yeshua when he was knocked off his horse and blinded by brilliant light. That got his attention, if nothing else would! Paul found out that day on the road to Damascus that Jesus sometimes introduces Himself in unorthodox ways! Speaking in Hebrew, according to Acts 26:14, Jesus asked why Paul had been persecuting Him. Now, there's a question that's hard to answer! But in typical Jewish fashion, Paul answered with another question: "Who are you, sir?"

A Voice From Heaven

And the voice from heaven said, *Ani Yeshua,* "I am Yeshua, whom you are persecuting." Paul had been intent on going to Damascus to gather up the Messianic Jews and bring them back to Jerusalem for punishment as heretics and troublemakers. But the Jewish Messiah, speaking in Hebrew, revealed Himself, in what Paul later called a heavenly vision. Even though Paul was to become the apostle to the Gentiles, he had a revelation of the Jewish, Hebrew-speaking Messiah that absolutely turned him around.

The Hebrew word for *repentance, t'shuvah,* means "to turn around." It is a poetic image of a man turning from one direction and going in a new direction. Repentance is not just regret; it is a complete change of direction. While once we were turned with our backs to God, when we repent we turn around so that God is always in front of us. This is what Paul meant when he later wrote that we should fix our eyes on Jesus. (See Hebrews 12:2.)

Dreams and visions have a way of changing our direction. God's plans for us can either be felt as promptings or pokings. That's why Yeshua said that Paul was having a hard time kicking against the goads. In Paul's day, oxen were directed with sharp pointed sticks called *goads.* When an ox needed to be turned, he was poked on one side, with the idea that the ox would turn away in discomfort and go in a different direction. When an ox did not wish to turn aside, he pushed back, kicking against the goads.

That is what Paul was doing each time the Holy Spirit pricked his conscience. And this is what I have done. I hate to admit how many "open doors" I have tried to walk through, only to bang my head against them when I discovered that the Lord had closed them. But in my own ox-like way, I tried to plow through anyway.

To change our direction, sometimes it takes dreams and visions—supernatural encounters with God that speak into those secret, otherwise unreachable parts of our lives. Once touched, somehow our rational minds are also affected, and our thinking changes. We *know* that we *know* that we *know*. . . .

GOD'S GOAD TO CHANGE MY THEOLOGY

For years I had served as a pastor among the Gentiles. In 1991 I began to stir with a hunger to discover more fully what God wanted of me as a Jew. In our church were many men and women who loved me and appreciated my Jewishness. But my own efforts to understand what God was doing among the Jewish people baffled or surprised my friends and congregants.

Sandy and I went to Israel in the fall of 1991, visited a number of Messianic congregations, met with Messianic leaders in several cities, and saw for ourselves what had developed in the decade since our first visit together to Israel. When we returned home to Rochester, New York, I was a different man.

I had led what we called an "Israel study group" for months and had come to the conclusion that there was much more to Romans 9–11 than I had previously understood. God's faithfulness to Israel, her irrevocable calling, and of course her stumbling were all things I had understood well. Only then did I realize that God's plan to restore the Jewish people was central to His End-Time plan for all of history.

For so long I had been among people with limited vision and understanding about Israel. Sandy had suppressed her enthusiasm for Israel and the Jewish people. I had tried to be cautious and diplomatic. Now, my theology was being reworked.

Since I was a child, I knew that God made the Jewish people for a special purpose. We were called to stand up for justice, to protect the oppressed, to right the wrongs of human society. If nothing else, we were called to be a voice of God, calling to a world, however deafened or disinterested.

Later as a disciple of Jesus, I knew that God wanted the Jewish people to be a light to the nations. And I knew that God had a great plan to revive and restore the Jewish people to Himself. What I didn't understand was that the restoration of the Jewish people was central to God's plan to make disciples of the nations.

Paul wrote to the Gentile Christians of Rome that they had benefited from Israel's historic failure to fully grasp and embrace the gospel of Yeshua. Though Israel stumbled over Yeshua, she would recover. After all, Paul knew Zechariah's prophecy that Israel would look upon Yeshua and mourn for Him, realizing that He was pierced for the Jewish people, wailing over Him as one grieves for a firstborn son (Zech. 12:10).

Paul wrote that when Israel recovered from the blindness that had prevented her from fully recognizing Messiah, it would be like bringing life from the dead. And he said it would be good for the Gentiles, for all nations of the world. He warned that the Gentiles must be neither ignorant nor arrogant, because they had a debt of love to the Jewish people. God loved the Jewish people, Paul wrote, because of His faithful love for the patriarchs, the fathers. Israel's irrevocable covenant was based on God's faithful response and love, not upon the Jewish people's own ability to be faithful and true. (See Romans 11:27.)

ECHOING THE PATRIARCHS

Paul expressed sentiments that are echoed in one of the most important prayers of the *siddur,* the Jewish prayer book. The *Shemoneh Esrei* (for its original eighteen declarations, benedictions, and petitions) or *Amidah* (because the prayer is said while standing) begins with a passage called *Ahvot,* "Fathers or Patriarchs." It declares that the Lord is our God and the God of our fathers—Abraham, Isaac, and Jacob. He is the great God, the mighty God, the fearful and awesome God. He is the Most High. He acts with kindness and remembers the covenant faithfulness and merciful love of the patriarchs. He treats the descendants of the patriarchs with kindness and love. He is the Creator and Purchaser of all. He redeems us, buying us back from slavery, and is our protection, the shield of Abraham.

Though the Jewish people are small in number, persecuted, stumbling spiritually, sometimes blind, sometimes obstinate, sometimes even rebellious, yet God loves us with an everlasting love. He loves us with *familial love.* Familial love is both undeserved and expansive, reaching past wrongs and sin, crossing the boundaries of generations. So is the love of the God and Father of Yeshua, the God and Father of Israel.

And God intends, Paul asserts, to save all Israel (Rom. 10:1). This whole process of Israel's recovery is mysterious, but it must be anticipated and appreciated by the nations. Life from the dead, Paul writes, is associated with Jewish revival. It is the principle of resurrection. And how much more will the *goyim,* the Gentile nations, be blessed when Israel recovers! (See Romans 11.)

MOVED BY THE HAND OF DESTINY

Sandy and I returned from Israel with a sense of destiny and wariness. On the Saturday before Christmas, I felt a particular need to be in the presence of God. We went to Congregation *Shema Yisrael,* the Messianic congregation led by my good friend, Jonathan Bernis. As we walked into the service, I heard the congregation singing Batya Segal's *Hodu L'adonai,* a song we had learned while in Israel. In Hebrew and English, it both calls and leads us into worship with the simple directive from the Psalms: *Hodu L'adonai key tov, key l'olam chasdoh.* "Give thanks to the Lord for He is good. His love forever endures." (See Psalm 107:1.) This had become a favorite song, and I interpreted it as a sign that we were in the right place.

Some time into worship, I had a thought about two ways

of praying. The first is a kind of petition. I remind God of promises and even pull verses out of context if necessary, trying to convince Him of the rightness of my request. It is as if I were trying to get His arm behind His back until He gives in and says, "Amen." The second prayer is born of listening. In my undemanding quietness, I hear God sharing with me what is on His heart. He gently waits for my "Amen."

As quickly as I had these thoughts, they came to an end when I realized I was thinking and should be worshiping. So I returned to the worship and joined in again with singing. Moments later, I had what I can only describe as a vision.

I was transported to a heavenly realm and stood in a place behind God the Father. From our vantage point, it was as if we were in outer space, on a faraway planet looking down upon the earth below. His hands were lifted up, and I heard Him speak one word. So loud was His voice that it went instantly from His realm to the earthly realm. Like the sound of a mighty waterfall or rolling thunder, His voice filled everything, yet it was not painful. It carried, it penetrated, but it was not like the high decibels of a rock concert or the shriek of feedback. The sound of His voice entered into things, and before my eyes I saw history unfolding.

In a cinematic vision, I saw a montage of modern Jewish history. Zionists in the late nineteenth and early twentieth centuries were traveling throughout Europe and Russia, gathering Jewish people to the land of Israel, the Palestine of the Turks and British. Waves of Jews moved toward the Promised Land. I saw the crowd assembled in Tel Aviv, in balconies and on the square, listening to the United Nations vote on Israel's Declaration of Independence in 1948. I saw Israel's Defense Forces storming into the old city of Jerusalem in 1967, liberating her ancient walls and sequestered Jewish inhabitants, reuniting her lovely stones under Jewish rule for the first time since Rome governed during the second temple era. I saw other fragments too.

Then I realized that God was speaking. With hands lifted up in the posture of the priests who bless, He was saying one word only: "Favor." He was speaking *favor to Zion,* and all these events, all these developments were the result of His heavenly pronouncement. *One word from God was shaping history!* One word proceeding from God's mouth to humanity was molding the future and the present.

I began to weep. Uncharacteristically, warm streams of tears cascaded down my cheeks. I was unembarrassed and unashamed, and I knew the tears must not be controlled. For so many years I had been trying to force God's hand, demanding, in a sense, that He bless my own strategy for Jewish revival. He hadn't, and again and again my efforts had failed miserably.

Now I realized what He had been doing for the last century, and my thoughts went back to those two kinds of prayer I had earlier been contemplating. I had been trying to get God to say *amen* to my prayers. Now here He was showing me what was on His heart, and I felt it was such a privilege.

To see and understand, to apprehend what God is doing in our world is one of the most satisfying experiences possible. It is awesome and undoing, as Isaiah declared, when he had a vision of God in the realm of His heavenly temple:

> In the year that king Uzziah died I saw also the Lord sitting upon a throne, high and lifted up, and his train filled the temple. . . . Then said I, Woe is me! for I am undone; because I am a man of unclean lips, and I dwell in the midst of a people of unclean lips: for mine eyes have seen the King, the LORD of hosts. Then flew one of the seraphims unto me, having a live coal in his hand, which he had taken with the tongs from off the altar: And he laid it upon my mouth, and said, Lo, this hath touched thy lips; and thine iniquity is taken away, and thy sin purged.
>
> —ISAIAH 6:1, 5–7

Then I heard the gentle voice of God's Spirit speaking to me in words marked with humor. "You know, I started without you . . ." He said, reminding me that the first wave of *aliyah* had begun about a century before. "And I can finish without you. *But you can help if you want.*"

It Costs Something

I smiled. I *could* help if I wanted. My choice. That afternoon, I went to my office and wrote a letter of resignation to my good friend and senior pastor, David Young. Our shared vision had been so substantial, but this vision, which was mine alone, would lead me onto a different path. I chose to serve my people, and I understood that the cost for me would include quitting my job, leaving the church, and joining the Messianic congregation.

It was one more time that dreams and visions had reached into the hidden recesses of hearts and souls, conveying direction and destiny far more powerfully than rational thought processes could allow. Only this time, the hearts and souls belonged to Sandy and me.

It took David several weeks to respond. My letter came in the midst of difficult times for us relationally. Was it the pain of conflict that prepared us for change? I have asked this many times about the numerous difficulties that surrounded that season of our lives. In retrospect, I realize that Sandy and I were unsettled, no doubt anxious and easily disturbed.

The prospect of change of this magnitude was almost unthinkable. We worked at repairing and recovering our relationship with the congregation we served in the name of love and respect. But it was thwarted by our differing destinations. Ultimately, we had to leave because we were headed now in different directions. Like fellow travelers who must part ways for the final leg of a journey, so we walked out of our lives in Cornerstone Christian Church, and into new lives at Congregation *Shema Yisrael*.

Sandy would later say it was like stepping off the corner of Meigs and Clinton, *and into the whole world.*

TATYANA

Tatyana's grandfather was a rabbi in Ukraine. Five years ago she moved to the United States. I met her at a Messianic synagogue where I had been speaking. This was her first visit to a Messianic congregation, and she was filled with questions. Tatyana's English was quite good, and her Russian accent was slight.

A few months earlier she had a series of dreams, which she told me about. In the first dream, Yeshua appeared to her as she was walking past a Catholic church. A priest stood in front of the building. As Tatyana looked carefully, pondering whether to enter, Yeshua said to her, "This is not for you."

In the second dream, Yeshua again appeared to her, this time as she was walking past a Russian Orthodox church. A priest stood in front of this building also. Again she considered entering, but Yeshua said to her, "This is not for you."

As she mediated on these two dreams, she was baffled. The Catholic and Russian Orthodox churches were the only expressions of Christianity that she knew. Then she had a third dream. In this, Yeshua appeared to her, and said simply, "Come, follow Me. I will show you where to go."

"I think Yeshua has brought me here," Tatyana told me. "I didn't even know there was such a thing as a Messianic synagogue."

A PEOPLE WHO DREAM

Tatyana's story is not unique. Regularly I meet people who have had similar dreams. It seems that we are living in a season in which Yeshua is appearing directly to Jewish people, revealing Himself, and calling them to be His disciples.

Dreams and visions are compelling to Jewish people, maybe to all people. We see so many cases in the Jewish Scriptures of how God revealed Himself or His will in a dream or a vision. Peter, the apostle to the Jews, cited a passage from the prophet Joel. In the name of the God of Israel, Joel prophesied that the Holy Spirit would be poured out on all flesh and blood, and that old men would dream dreams and young men would see visions. (See Joel 2:28; Acts 2:17.)

The record of the apostles is consistent with the *Tanakh* in describing significant dreams and visions from God. In our day, as favor is again being poured out on Zion and the Holy Spirit is again being poured out on the Jewish people, dreams and visions are returning.

Avi Mizrachi is a second-generation Messianic Jew, living in Israel. His mother was the secretary to Rabbi Daniel Zion, a highly regarded spiritual leader from Bulgaria. Yeshua appeared to Rabbi Zion, and almost everyone in his congregation became a disciple of Yeshua. The community made *aliyah,* settling in Yaffa, the port next to Tel Aviv, in the very city where Peter had had his vision about the unclean animals. Rabbi Zion continued in the traditions of his forefathers, leading an Israeli synagogue, but including Yeshua in everything that he did.

Messianic Jews value their Jewish identity and lifestyles, finding deep spiritual meaning and importance as they include Yeshua in the center of their lives. Almost two thousand years ago, a controversy swirled in Israel among the followers of Yeshua. Was it possible for non-Jews to be saved without converting to Judaism? For most of the last seventeen centuries the mirror of the controversy has been raging. Is it possible for Jews to be saved without departing from their Judaism?

Tatyana and Rabbi Zion are two examples of Jews who have had direct supernatural encounters with the Messiah of Israel, but were directed to preserve their Jewish identities, remaining within the Jewish community. Yeshua himself was so fully a Jew, we can learn from his example.

YESHUA'S JEWISH HERITAGE SPEAKS YET TODAY

He was born a Jew, circumcised on the eighth day, and redeemed as a firstborn son according to the commandments of *Pidyon HaBen.* His parents, both Jewish, were born in Israel and were observant enough to travel to Jerusalem for Passover each year. In a time when Roman and Greek culture drew many out of their Jewishness, Joseph and Mary, or better, Yosef and Miryam, chose to continue with a Jewish identity and to pass it on to their son.

Yeshua was accustomed to celebrating *Shabbat* in the synagogue and was comfortable being called up for the public reading of the Scriptures. He taught about what was permitted on *Shabbat,* took positions on the weighty commandments (loving God and our neighbors) and the less weighty (tithing), and dialogued with men of influence and learning from the various schools of Jewish thought.

Yeshua placed a great emphasis on the *Tanakh,* and after His Resurrection, He opened the minds of His disciples so that they could rightly understand the Jewish Scriptures. He was also familiar with the oral *Torah* and the various traditions and strands of Judaism.

Even after His Ascension into heaven, the glorified, resurrected Messiah spoke Hebrew, identifying Himself to Paul by saying, *Ani Yeshua,* "I am Yeshua."

When I first encountered Messianic Jews, I thought their use of the name Yeshua was an affectation. That only changed when I more fully realized Yeshua's essential Jewish identity. As a Bible lover, I couldn't strip away His Jewishness without disregarding major portions of Scripture. In fact, I could only pay true respect, both to the Scriptures and to Yeshua Himself, by esteeming and appreciating His Jewishness more fully.

I have concluded that it is possible to embrace Yeshua, keeping Him at the center of my life, while at the same time embracing my Jewishness. I once was afraid that Jewishness might inherently include a tendency toward legalism. I no longer think this is true. When I more fully and intimately discovered the living Jewishness of Yeshua, realizing that He was more observant than I was, I determined that I could live as a Jew. In fact, Yeshua is my pattern. I want to be the kind of Jew He was. To be His disciple means to follow Him, imitating Him in a sense. As a Jew, I can actively choose a Jewish lifestyle that reflects the lifestyle of Yeshua. I can live as a Jew and as a disciple of Yeshua without tension or identity crisis. Both can contribute meaningfully to the other.

This then required a new kind of relationship. I had come to know Him intimately as Jesus. It was time to know Him intimately as Yeshua. Yeshua is at the very center of the life of every Messianic Jew. If I move Him out of the center, I destroy the Messianic Jewish way of life. Only when my eyes are fixed on Him can I clearly see the rest of my Jewishness. All of my Jewishness is brought into focus by my understanding of who Yeshua is and how I am to relate to Him as Lord and Savior.

THE JEWISH ROOT RESTORED TO CHRISTIANITY

Not only is the Jewishness of Yeshua being restored, and the Jewish identities of Jewish believers, but the Jewish root of Christian faith is also being restored. The root is Jewish for two reasons. First, the root is Yeshua Himself, who was born a Jew, died a Jew, and has chosen an eternal identity as a Jew. He used His Jewish lifestyle as the framework for discipling those who would follow Him. So he is no doubt thoroughly Jewish. Even after His resurrection, He showed us that He continued in His Jewish identity. Speaking to Paul in Hebrew, the resurrected, glorified, ascended Messiah identified Himself by saying, *Ani Yeshua*, "I am Yeshua." Showing Himself in the eternal realm, He is identified in Revelation as the Lion of the tribe of Judah. He is the vine. He is Jewish, and we—whether Jew or non-Jew—are grafted into Him as branches.

The root is also Jewish because it is true to the faith of the patriarchs. As believers, we follow the pattern of the patriarchs, expecting a direct relationship with a living God, experiencing Him, learning of His ways, and walking faithfully with Him to the end of our days. It is for the sake of the root—the patriarchs—that Israel's calling is irrevocable and will lead to her full redemption. (See Romans 11.) So we honor the fathers of faith by loving the sons and daughters of Israel.

When the Jewish root thrives, so will all the branches. This is a principle of horticulture and agriculture—and of the spiritual realm. When the root withers, the entire tree dies. As the Christian church comes to terms with the Jewish root of its faith, embracing it with love and respect, the church will be blessed. This is guaranteed.

Dreams of Yeshua

Yeshua appeared in a dream recently to a young Israeli serving in the armed forces. He not only revealed Himself to this young man, He also told him he would meet someone on the streets of Tel Aviv who would tell him more. A grandson of an Israeli rabbi, the young man encountered a Messianic Jew who was participating in an outreach on the streets of Tel Aviv. There he heard the Jewish gospel clearly. In witness to his response to the gospel message, Avi Mizrachi presided over his *mikveh,* his immersion in water, in the name of Yeshua.

Friends who knew I was writing this book have reported to me similar life-changing encounters that people they know have had with Yeshua in their dreams. Yeshua appeared in a vision—"He came into my room," they typically say—to countless Jews in the last few years. These supernatural experiences are transforming people, touching hearts, and changing minds in a way that no rational encounter could.

This is not to take away from the value of dialogue, the sharing of the gospel, or intelligent, rational discussion. It is simply to agree with how God is choosing to reach some people in these days. After all, if God can reach Moses through a burning bush, I guess He can decide exactly how best to reach every one of us.

I have met many Jews who, like myself, discovered the God of Israel and His Messiah through an encounter with a faithful Gentile. How wonderful it is when these disciples point us in the direction of our own people too!

Messianic synagogues have profound significance in that they allow Jewish believers to fully develop both as believers and as Jews. Nowhere else can we more successfully explore the issues of our Jewishness and faith. In Messianic congregations, we can pass on Jewish lifestyle and identity to our children and remain a visible, identifiably faithful Jewish remnant.

Now, I don't think that all Jewish believers belong in Messianic congregations, nor do I think that Messianic congregations are the only true expression of biblical faith. For years I understood almost everything essential to the Messianic vision except for the value and necessity of Messianic congregations. No wonder, then, that I found myself a Jew ministering in a non-Jewish setting, thinking that people like Jonathan Bernis were off the mark. I now believe that the future of Jewish ministry belongs to Messianic congregations and that they can partner with fellow Gentile believers in the churches.

But of one thing, I am also certain: The restoration of the Jewish people, bringing life from the dead, will help bring wonderful blessing to all the nations. It is in the interest of the Gentile nations to learn to bless the Jewish people. As they do this, they will also be blessed.

הדרך

HaDerekh

• •

More than the Jews have kept the Sabbath,
the Sabbath has kept the Jews.
— The early Zionist leader and
theoretician, Ahad Ha'am (1856–1927)

CHAPTER
THREE

IT TOOK MANY YEARS FOR MY FAMILY TO RECOVER FROM THE SHOCK of my decisive turn toward Jesus. During that first period, we learned not even to discuss the issue of my faith. But later, all of our hearts softened toward one another, and the familial bond showed itself capable of enduring such tension and trouble.

As children, Rhona, my younger sister, and I played together the most. But from adolescence my older sister, Karen, and I were the closest of my five siblings, and together we shared many matters of the heart. For my earliest years as a believer, I suffered for the loss of this intimacy, and I looked to my wife and other female friends for Karen's virtues and friendship, which at the time were not accessible to me.

I remember the day, but not the year, when Karen was ready to talk about the once-taboo subject of my faith. Karen is an attorney by education and a poet by temperament, articulate and insightful, penetrating but not argumentative by nature. When she opened the conversation, it reopened a chapter of love and dialogue that continues to this day.

It is true that our thoughts about Yeshua were vastly different, but that was not all that had separated us. I was different now, I told Karen, first because of what I believe about God. As Jews, we were both familiar with synagogue life and the Conservative Jewish way of praying. A little

Hebrew, a little English, some more Hebrew, sometimes sprinting, sometimes lagging behind, sometimes dragging our way through the synagogue service as each person, only sporadically in sync with the others, made his or her own way through the *Siddur,* the Jewish prayer book. In a theoretical sense we all believed in miracles. If God could distinguish what each one was saying in the cacophony of our unsynchronized praying, then He could do anything.

We knew that it was normal to go to our synagogue and pray. We speak to God, yes, we do. And we would pray and chant and sing to God, though in our synagogue we never sang very well. Though we thought it was possible to speak to God, it wasn't until much later that I learned that He actually listens. He hears us, and He responds; in fact, He speaks back to us.

The first division in our relationship occurred when I told Karen: "I have faith, a trusting relationship with the God of Israel, not because I have leapt off the cliff of reason into the abyss of religion. Rather, I have become more reasonable than ever. I have faith because I have heard God, and found He speaks the truth with love. I have relied on His guidance and found He is trustworthy."

"How can I know . . . ?" I had asked Pat Pritchard when I first met him in 1976.

"Pray," he had told me. "Pray specifically. The more specific the better. And when God answers, you'll know."

I remember praying privately because it was a private matter between God and me.

"God, I know You exist. But this Jesus, I don't know about Him. If He's real, I want to know, and I'll act appropriately. And if He's not, well, please pardon me for asking, but I need to get this settled." I prayed this sincerely, concluding with, "Amen." A simple prayer, from my heart to God. I spoke to Him, and I really did expect a response. This expectation of His responsiveness was based on my presupposition of His reality. I later memorized a verse that helped provoke me: "Without faith it is impossible to please him: for he that cometh to God must believe that he is, and that he is a rewarder of them that diligently seek him" (Heb. 11:6).

TO SEEK BY SEEKING

This was the first time in my life when I was diligently seeking God. I had previously been curious, but this was different. One of the ways that the Hebrew language expresses diligence is by doubling, or repeating, a verb. To diligently seek is expressed in the Hebrew idiom, "to seek by seeking." Many people think about seeking God. They may contemplate the idea of God or ruminate about the things they have heard about Him. Some take college courses in theology or philosophy or try in some other way to learn answers to their most fundamental questions about God. But the Bible advises that we will find God only when we seek Him with all our heart (Deut. 4:29). In other words, we must seek God by actually seeking Him, as the doubled verb implies.

When I prayed to God, it was because I was seeking Him. I *did* expect to find Him. I wasn't speaking into the air. Prayer, after all, is not a soliloquy, a dramatic speech, a device to attract an audience. Prayer is nothing less than talking to the living God. We pray *because He is there listening*.

One day, not more than two weeks later, I was again by myself, and I heard a voice from heaven, a spiritual voice. I don't know if the voice spoke in a way that others could hear, but it didn't matter since I was alone.

What *did* matter was that I *heard* Him. I heard my name called out, repeated. "David, David." A voice of love, of tenderness, and a voice I loved. Somehow, I immediately understood that *this* was the voice of Jesus, speaking by the Holy Spirit, the voice of God Himself. Something about that voice—I don't know what—conveyed an instantaneous understanding, and with it a transformation. My spirit, I now understood, had been dead but was now revived. As Jesus had said, I was being born again.

When God spoke my name, He showed that He knew me, knew me personally by name. I was not a statistic or just another human being to be addressed anonymously and impersonally, as if to say, "Hey, you!" The way God spoke made me understand instantly that He loved me. This was not the God of philosophy; He was not abstract, not intellectual. This was the personal God, the living God, the one true God. Faith came to me at that moment. I don't mean that I became religious or observant. I simply mean that faith—trusting and loving God—came to me the instant that I first heard His voice. "Faith," the Bible says, "cometh by hearing, and hearing by the word of God" (Rom. 10:17).

Now I know that there are many doors that open onto paths of discovering God, but every one of them, I have found, requires that we go through the door of Yeshua, Jesus. No one comes to the Father except through Him (John 14:6). That's why Yeshua described Himself as the Way, *HaDerekh,* "the way or path or even the road."

When I heard God, I was transformed. And I knew something for sure: We can pray, and God does answer. His answers may come to us powerfully through words. This is why the Jewish prophets said so frequently, "The word of the Lord came to me, saying . . . "

Praying is something that we Jews thought normal. Hearing God, on the other hand, was not. It was unusual, even strange, to suggest that God Himself would speak back to us. Karen and I amused ourselves with the thought of going to synagogue for a *Shabbat* service, and actually hearing a voice, the voice of the Lord, speak out to the congregation amid the cacophony of all our praying. How shocked everyone would be, we agreed. And yet at a personal level, this very thing had happened to me—God spoke to me. It shocked me indeed. I was forever changed by two things: first, that God spoke, and second, by what He revealed.

CONVERSATIONS WITH GOD

If I had been raised as a Jew, it was not as a mystic. I don't remember that anyone in my family ever spoke about their own conversations with God. As a ten-year-old, I do remember walking around Fort McHenry in the Baltimore harbor, asking my aunt questions about God. Though I heard nothing memorable, the conversation did encourage me to keep asking, if not to this aunt, then at least to other people. I went to synagogue, to Hebrew school, prepared for my *Bar Mitzvah,* and studied for my confirmation. And in our classes we talked about God, but not about our own relationships with Him. We prayed, but rarely, and even more rarely from the center of our hearts. And never did two of us gather together and simply talk with God. Never did we pray with the expectation that God would speak back to us. And absolutely never did we pray with the thought that He would reveal Himself as Yeshua.

Though I was looking for God, I had come across Jesus. At first this seemed inconvenient, then troublesome. Though I was taught we Jews had no dogma, we really did—and the central point of our catechism was this: Jews do not believe in Jesus.

So the unthinkable had happened. I was changed, and it was irreversible. I think for many years my father harbored a secret wish that one day I would phone him and announce that it had all been a mistake. I had come back to my senses, recanting my faith in Yeshua. But that never happened, and my father is now gone.

Dad died, I am sure, with acceptance of my faith, though not with agreement. But his heart certainly had opened to the God of the Jewish people, and that can only mean that Yeshua had opened the door, because no one can come to God, the Father of the Jewish people, without help from the Son. I hope, of course, that during those last moments of life, the unknowable bridge between this life and the realm of the eternal, my father might have seen who was in fact standing at the door, opening it. If so, I'm sure he would have been shocked, even perplexed, but I think he would have recovered from the surprise and enjoyed the serendipity of it all.

Dad loved serendipitous things. He traveled regularly on business, the owner and general manager of a prosperous radio station (until the advent of FM stereo and the decline of AM radio). Often he would come home from work or from a business trip and tell me of some unexpected joy he had experienced. "Hope for the best, but prepare for the worst," he would say. He wasn't advocating optimism or positive thinking, but genuine hope. And so, not as a Pollyanna, but as the son of my *father* and the son of my *Father,* I hope that Dad encountered Yeshua at the door to eternity.

Imagine the glorified Messiah, the Consolation of Israel, reaching out to take my father's hand. "Come to me," He has said, "all ye that . . . are heavy laden, and I will give you rest" (Matt. 11:28). I can only hope that my father stretched forth his own hand and placed it in Yeshua's to cross the portals of eternity *yad l'yad,* "hand in hand."

The God of Miracles

"A second thing I believe," I told my sister, "is that God works miracles because His realm is supernatural. Yes, God heals the sick."

"Then what about our mother?" Karen would ask. Mom had been sick, bedridden, for eleven years, once comatose after a weak blood vessel leaked in her brain in 1983. She could have died at that time, I knew, because my friend Don Mahana had died from a brain aneurysm not long before.

Don had fallen away from the Lord in a way that forced me to disfellowship him. But one Sunday years later, he sought me out, repentant, humble, contrite, as much in need of God as anyone I had known. And he was aware of that need, desperately so. We counseled together, his marriage all but destroyed, and we prayed together. And God did something that very day, bringing a threefold reconciliation—Don with me, Don with his wife, and Don with the Lord.

The very next morning the phone rang, and I heard Barbara, Don's wife, crying hysterically. Don was in the backyard, fallen, stricken. They lived just three blocks away, and I arrived before the ambulance. Don was lying in the yard, unresponsive, his breathing labored, his eyes glassy, his mouth gurgling. At the hospital we found out that a little blood had burst from a weakened vessel in his brain. He had passed out, vomited, and aspirated his vomit. Oxygen had been choked off from his brain at a time when it was most needed, and a few days later he was pronounced brain dead.

Don's parents came immediately upon his hospitalization, and together with Barbara made the necessary but tragic decision to remove his life support. We had seen his EEGs, and several of us intuitively recognized that Don's body had been left vacant already, as if his soul had already taken leave, returning to his God. Just in time he had received that marvelous gift of repentance, and though it led only to eternal life, it was life nevertheless.

But my mother did not die after her aneurysm. She lived on, with no real medical hope for recovery. Almost completely paralyzed, her left arm and hand had to be restrained to protect her from pulling out her feeding tube. Her head would rest upon that nursing-home pillow, black hair slowly turning to gray over the years, teeth deteriorating, never again able to read or speak.

I remember dreams of Mom getting out of bed, recovering slowly, joining her beloved family. In one dream, we drove to the Pennsylvania towns of her youth, retracing the places of her earliest memories, hoping to somehow reconstruct or renew thoughts and feelings, a person grown feeble with disuse. These dreams sparked hope and prayer that she would awaken from her coma, recover from her brain damage, and be physically restored, but Mom never left that hospital bed as I had hoped . . . dreamed.

The beginning of her tragedy is still fresh to me, though some details have been reworked unconsciously or lost. Mom, Dad, and I were sitting around my parents' breakfast table, looking out onto a panorama of several acres of woods that surrounded their seven-thousand-square-foot home. My parents were partners together in a radio station, WROV-AM 1240, and I worked with them for many years.

As we discussed a particularly vexing employee, Mom put her head in her hands. My father and I thought she was exasperated, if not with the employee, then with us. This was our weekly management meeting, and maybe the pressure on Mom was too great.

She slumped further, then fell out of her chair. Something was terribly wrong. Dad asked me to call the rescue squad. He was distressed, calmly worried. He tried to do anything, but he could really do nothing but talk to his wife as she lay on the floor. I gave the rescue squad directions to my parents' house, then called my wife. I asked Sandy to hurry and meet the ambulance at the foot of the driveway because the house was hidden behind another, sharing a driveway as a private road.

I prayed over my mom, aware that what was happening to her was like what had happened to Don. In unknown tongues I prayed, disregarding the theological distance between my dad and me. This was not a time for discretion.

As Sandy arrived, even before the rescue squad had entered the room, a green cast of death fell upon my mother. With the pallor and grip of death so visible, the presence of death so palpable, the Holy Spirit whispered a secret: This was a *spirit of death,* and Sandy and I must rebuke it. When we did, her color returned, along with her breathing, and we knew that at that very moment God had miraculously saved her life. God's salvation sometimes follows a pattern we can call "first the natural, then the spiritual." God had saved my mother from physical death, this we saw.

Later in the hospital she recovered enough strength to speak a few words, but her vital signs indicated that her recovery was superficial and would not last for long. All of my siblings rushed in from their homes—my brother Marc from Boston, sister Karen from Florida, others from nearby.

One day, still in intensive care, she was rejecting the respirator. Her physician gathered the family to explain to us the likely events. If he left the respirator attached, it would kill her, so he had no choice but to remove it. And when he did, he could expect that her breathing would be labored and insufficient. He described the sequence in which her various systems and functions would fail. She would die soon, he told us.

We all began to weep, some silently, some quietly, gasps and moans and sounds too loud to be called sighs. Our beloved mother, helpless at fifty-three years old. We held one another, hugged in turns, arms reaching to gather in those whose presence we knew but couldn't see for the tears clouding our eyes. Rivers of tears ran hot down my cheeks, mourning, agonizing, anticipating, incapable of reversing this death sentence. And in the midst of this helpless, hopeless situation, love flowed as each of us held each other—first one, then another, holding and being held.

The doctor carried out his duties, but to his surprise Mom gasped, then breathed, and kept on breathing. And she kept on living. How can you explain this act of mourning the dead before they are dead, only to find they are still alive, not like before, but alive still?

He Who Raises the Dead

We Jews have a prayer, the *Shemoneh Esrei,* or "Eighteen." Originally divided into its eighteen sections (one extra section was added later), this prayer is said while standing; thus it is also known as the *Amidah.* It begins with a section called *Ahvot,* or "Fathers," because it is a reminder to God and ourselves that we are descendants of His faithful ones, Abraham, Isaac, and Jacob. In Romans 11:27, Paul echoes this sentiment, declaring that the Jewish people are loved for the sake of the patriarchs.

The second section, *Gibor*, focuses on God's power and might. But the terms do not indicate human power like that of a king or a president with their armies and weapons of destruction. God's power is not shown in His ability to destroy, but in His ability to make right. His is the power to heal and revive. *Atah gibor l'olam Adonai, makhayay may-teem, atah rav l'hosheeah.* "You are mighty forever, my Lord, who raises the dead; you are mighty to save." *Somaykh noflim, v'rophe kholim.* "You lift up the falling and heal the sick."

The Jewish prayer for the dead, the Mourner's *Kaddish,* makes no mention of death. In fact, it is a declaration of praise and adoration for God; it even says that He is above every praise and act of worship we can make with our words and deeds. It begins *Yitgadal,* "magnified," then continues with words that Yeshua borrowed to include in the prayer He gave His disciples known now as the Lord's prayer: *v'Yitkadash shamay rabbah,* "Sanctified is His great name/hallowed be His name."

Here was my mother, twice almost dead, still failing, still sick, but alive. Let His great name be magnified and sanctified, even as Mom lay there.

Each of her six children, their spouses, her parents, and other relatives took turns visiting with her. Sandy and I would take our turns with Mom, seeing her privately. We would pray over her stricken body, but see no changes. Mom went to a specialized facility for head injuries in Boston, but even with their best efforts, she did not recover. Eventually she returned, destined for residency in a nursing home.

When Sandy and I would pray for Mom during this period, her face would change horribly. At the mention of Jesus, her face would contort. She would grind her teeth and shake her head violently from side to side. Her face would turn red, fit with anger, hostility, and protest. The blood vessels on her temples would pop out, pulsing with rage. Despite her affliction, Mom still could make her position known. It was almost demonic; maybe it was simply that. In any case, we were disheartened, until one day when the Lord spoke to Sandy.

"Why do you think I am limited by what you call cognitive awareness?" the Lord asked.

This birthed genuine faith in us. There are many attitudes of prayer, but few are as glorious as the prayer of faith, which produces a genuine breakthrough. Different from a petition, we are no longer asking for something. It is as if we have already received our request and are filled with thanksgiving for the request having been granted. We are thanking God, not in expectation as if there is yet any delay or contingency that must be met. It is as if we were transferred into God's realm and see things completed from the perspective of eternity. Still, to the naked, natural eye, there is no change. It is not wishful thinking or even anticipation. It is not the claim of a promise. In our spiritual senses, the matter is already done, and we have the sense and experience that this is true. So it was with Mom.

We knew that God had broken through—not that He would, but that He had. Our attitude and demeanor changed. And when we next visited and prayed for Mom, a marvelous change was visible. At the name of the Lord, Jesus, she smiled. We prayed in tongues, and she grinned.

Though the years stretched on and her body never recovered, more changes took place at the spiritual level. Sandy and I had moved to Rochester, New York, and when we would visit, we would worship and pray in Mom's presence. There were times when the presence of the Lord was pure and glorious. Sometimes we would alternate between smiling and crying. Tears of joy would flow down Mom's cheeks when we were together, worshiping.

In the winter of 1991–92, my family was supportive of our decision to leave the Christian church we were a part of and to join the Messianic movement. Karen had difficulty relating to me in my role as pastor, but not so as a Messianic rabbi. Perhaps this made more sense to her Jewish mind, and to mine as well.

In 1994, Mom's condition deteriorated, and there were moments when we all began to understand that her end was near. On my birthday, September 13, 1994, Karen, Dad, and I went to visit Mom. It was the last time I saw her. Karen asked if I would go with her and Dad to see Mom and to pray together. I brought my *siddur* and opened to the *Shema,* chanting it in the way known to Jews all over the world. The presence of God fell, and the four of us began to weep together, sorrow and joy alternating. This is the way of life, and the way of the Lord. "Blessed are those who mourn; they will be comforted." There we were—me a Messianic, my sister and father Conservative Jews, and my mom—indescribably experiencing the Eternal One together.

Sandy and I went to Kiev for one of Hear O Israel's festivals. The last night of the festival was a Saturday, and when it was over we returned to our hotel, a former Soviet Intourist facility. Our rooms were frosty and without heat. Headed for the dining room, I received a call on my walkie-talkie from Jonathan Bernis. Mom had died, and Karen was on the phone. Could I come to his room to talk with Karen? During the weeks of our absence, Mom's condition had worsened still, with several terrible convulsive, thrashing episodes. Karen peacefully told me the sad news, and we talked about the funeral. Jewish funerals are normally scheduled quickly, and embalming is rarely chosen. But Mom's sister lived in Paris, and with our distance, the funeral would wait a few days for all us to arrive.

I went to my room and wept for hours. How can a son express the sorrow of the loss of the woman who brought him forth? A child must mourn for a parent with special care, and in an extended way, we Jews learn. Again hot rivers of tears cascaded down my cheeks, wetting my shirt and my hands, which I instinctively cupped over my eyes.

Sandy and I hurried to Virginia for the funeral. I was asked to bring the eulogy. I wrote it on the plane, and rehearsed it for my dad and Karen. At Beth Israel, the synagogue of my youth, I spoke from the pulpit those words of love and affection for my mom and for the Lord who had given her life and sustained her and our family all those years.

Everyone in the community knew we had come from overseas, and many were interested in talking to us about what we were doing and about our ministry in the former Soviet Union. There was much curiosity, discussion, and questions, all of it temperate and polite.

Dad died just half a year later of stomach cancer, like his elder brother, Ben. Again I brought the eulogy, again at Beth Israel Synagogue. It's a sad thing to bury the dead, sadder still to bury your parents and both so soon together.

Jews repeat Job's words each time we bury our loved ones: "The LORD gave, and the LORD hath taken away; blessed be the name of the LORD" (Job 1:21). At the grave, we each take turns shoveling the dirt upon the lowered casket, confronting our own short spans, hearts beckoning for the eternal.

THE SPIRIT WHO REVIVES

"I have called thee by thy name; thou art mine" (Isa. 43:1).

By the time my grandmother Mary was born in Russia, all of our Jewish family memories were rooted in that part of the world. I am of the tribe of Levi, a ministering, priestly tribe. My father, Burton Levine, was a Levite. His father, Maurice Levine, was a Levite. And back we go. But we have lost track of when our ancestors left Babylon after the exile from Israel and of when they wandered into the land of the North, ending up in Russia.

While Herzl was igniting the fires of Zionism all over Europe, the troubles of the Jewish people in Eastern Europe and Russia grew worse. It was a time of political instability, with constantly changing borders, as Poland, Austria, Hungary, Russia, Romania, Bessarabia, and other countries vied for land they thought was their own and for power they thought they deserved. There's a wonderful Jewish joke from that time period.

After one particularly prolonged battle, the Russians were victorious over the Poles. A young Jewish man returned home to tell his family the news. Inside their simple wooden cabin, he found only his elderly grandmother. "*Bube*, Grandmother," he said. "I have important news. We don't live in Poland anymore! We live in Russia!"

"Praise God," she responded, as a smile of simple pleasure came over her face. "I was getting so tired of those hard Polish winters."

This period was a time of great trouble for the Jewish people. The political changes often brought with them sudden difficulties. Jews were attacked, wounded, raped, and murdered in bloodthirsty assaults known as *pogroms*.

At the same time the vision for Zionism was spreading, the sorrows of the *pogroms* and the fearful uncertainties of the future led hundreds of thousands of Jews to flee for their lives. Many went to Israel, and many more went westward.

My grandmother Mary was ten years old when she, along with some others from her Russian Jewish village, began to walk toward the ports of Europe, hoping to find a ship that would ferry her to New York.

She came across the Atlantic on a ship laden with bunks made of simple, unpadded wooden planks, so many shelves, each with its own layer of humanity. Jewish children like her, some fractured families, and even some whole families with their multiple generations, crammed themselves into these tiny crowded, uncomfortable places because they had a dream of surviving, of living, of freedom.

Grandma Mary never lost her Russian accent in this new land. Her life was preserved here in the United States. Though six million Jews lost their lives in Hitler's assault in

Europe and Russia, all my grandparents had escaped to the United States.

In 1994 I was in Moscow, in the "new" Russia, but still the Russia of my ancestors. There I would meet hundreds of other Jewish people, many my own age, others old enough to have been alive during the Holocaust. These were the Russian Jews whose grandparents had not left for Israel or for the United States. These were the children of the survivors. And I fell in love with them.

מה עושים עם ישוע?

WHAT DO WE DO WITH YESHUA?

••

Every dispute that is for a heavenly cause will ultimately endure.
— ETHICS OF THE FATHERS 5:17

CHAPTER
FOUR

IMAGINE A SIX-POINTED JEWISH STAR, THE MAGEN DAVID, AND IN
the middle is written *Yeshua*. This is a graphic picture of the
character of Messianic Judaism. It is Jewishness with Yeshua
at the center.

When we Messianic Jews are healthy and mature, Yeshua
is at the core of our lives individually and congregationally.
We are focused on Yeshua, and this is what makes us different from all other forms of faith within the Jewish
community. Centering on Yeshua Himself is what distinguishes us from every other kind of synagogue. Expressing
our faith in a Jewish way distinguishes us from Gentile
Christians.

Messianic Judaism traces its origins to the first century
when thousands of Jewish people put their trust in Yeshua.
First in Israel, then in the *Diaspora,* these disciples formed
Messianic synagogues where Yeshua was worshiped. In
time, the Jewish apostles also shared the good news of
Yeshua with Gentiles, and they too joined the Messianic
congregations. Though Gentile disciples would eventually
outnumber Jewish disciples, it is historically true that the
Christianity we know today emerged from a Jewish milieu,
and in its earliest form it was simply a branch of the varie-
gated Judaism of the second Temple era. The roots of
Christianity are decidedly Jewish. Messianic Judaism began
from that Jewish root and has returned in this modern era

as a restoration movement—not as a novelty or a recent invention—recovering what was lost so many years ago.

A Tragic Mistake

We believe it was a tragic mistake for the Gentile Christians to separate themselves from the Jewish roots of their faith. In his letter to the Romans, the apostle Paul warned the Gentile Christians about this error, and counseled them to remember that God's calling of the Jewish people was irrevocable. He cautioned the Gentiles not to be either ignorant or arrogant about the Jewish people. Yet in A.D. 325 the Gentile Christian Council of Nicea formally passed Christian law making it illegal for Jewish believers to be faithful to their Jewish heritage, calling, identity, and lifestyle.

Circumcision of sons, commanded to Abraham to take place on the eighth day, was banned for Jewish believers. This ban began despite the fact that circumcision predated the Sinai covenant and Mosaic law. It ignored the fact that Yeshua was circumcised on the eighth day, putting on His human body the permanent sign of identification with the Jewish people. And it ignored the fact that Paul insisted that his protegé, Timothy, be circumcised at the very same time as he was relaying the apostolic conclusion that Gentile disciples must not be compelled to be circumcised.

The celebration of *Shabbat* on Saturday (or more correctly, from Friday sundown until Saturday sundown) was also forbidden despite the fact that the *Shabbat* was included in the Ten Commandments, both in the Exodus and Deuteronomy versions. It ignored the fact that *Shabbat* was associated with God's rest on the seventh day and the rest withheld from the Jews during the period of their enslavement in Egypt. *Shabbat* preceded the Jerusalem temple and its rituals. By forbidding *Shabbat* on Saturday, the Nicean Council was also ignoring Yeshua's custom of attending synagogue on Saturdays, teaching from the *Torah* and Prophets. The council also disregarded the history of the earliest followers of Yeshua, who met in homes, synagogues, and the temple. And the council ignored Paul's custom of going first to the Jews with the gospel and speaking in synagogues and teaching on the *Shabbat*. This was done simply to separate the Christians from the Jews, with the Christians choosing Sunday as their communal day of worship.

The celebration of Passover according to the biblical calendar and traditions was also forbidden. A careful reckoning was made so that Easter and Passover would not coincide. This was one of many steps taken to disconnect Christian traditions from biblical Jewish traditions.

Finally, Jewish disciples were forced to renounce their Jewishness and to have no common fellowship with rabbinic or secular Jews. This cut off Jewish disciples from their families, friends, and community. Strangely, on this matter the Gentile church leaders and the chief rabbis were agreed. Though they disagreed about the person and nature of Yeshua, they were of one mind regarding Jews who believed in Yeshua. Perversely, both wanted to rid the world of identifiable Jewish disciples of Yeshua. And so they nearly did.

From A.D. 325 until this last century, Jews who chose to follow Yeshua were assimilated into the greater Gentile Christian world, abandoning their Jewish people. Such Jews believed they were no longer Jewish; they set aside their Jewish lifestyles and identities. They did not raise their children as Jews, but as Christians. It would only take one generation to wipe out the visible Jewish identity, but even so God had a plan to restore a visible, faithful remnant of Jews who trusted in Yeshua.

THE JEWISH YESHUA

Joseph Rabinowitz lived in Kishnev, Moldova, in the late 1800s. On a trip to Israel, he had a spiritual experience of Yeshua. While praying on the Mount of Olives, looking down on the temple mount, Rabinowitz had a vision and discovered the promised Jewish Messiah. He realized that not only was Yeshua promised to the Jewish people, but Yeshua was *Jewish Himself.*

The understanding of Yeshua's Jewish identity affected Rabinowitz deeply and permanently. He considered Yeshua the elder brother of the Jewish people. Rabinowitz understood the compatibility of Jewishness and faith in Yeshua. He chose to continue in his Jewish lifestyle, refusing to forsake his Jewish identity.

He became the darling of many evangelicals, including some of the earliest modern Christian Zionists like the great scholar Franz Delitzch, who translated the New Testament into Hebrew, cowrote an important Old Testament commentary, and loved the Jewish people, advocating evangelism directed to them.

On one hand, many of Rabinowitz's friends were encouraged that he was visibly Jewish and successfully preaching to the Jewish people. They helped him financially in his mission to the Jewish people, helping him to build a prayer house for the Jewish believers. He named it *Beit Lechem*—Bethlehem—"House of Bread." There Rabinowitz would preach a distinctively Jewish gospel to a primarily Jewish audience. His reputation as an evangelist to the Jews grew along with his effectiveness.

But on the other hand many Gentile Christian supporters were suspicious of Rabinowitz's emphasis on a continuing Jewish lifestyle and identity. It was fine for Jews to become disciples, but eventually, it was thought, they should not need their Jewishness any longer and could fit within the Christian churches. Rabinowitz insisted otherwise. If Yeshua was Jewish, if His apostles were Jewish, then modern Jews could also retain their Jewishness as they became disciples.

Some denominational support for Rabinowitz dwindled as it became clear that he would not soon abandon his Jewishness in order to come into a Christian denominational fold. But Delitzch and others stood by Rabinowitz, giving him the latitude to determine how best to live as a Jewish believer. In a very real sense, Rabinowitz became the father of modern Messianic Judaism, with the focus on the centrality of Yeshua and the emphasis on a continuing Jewish lifestyle and identity.

COMINGLING THEN, AS NOW

At times, though, compromise was struck, and Gentile Christian elements were mingled with the Jewish. Such comingling continues to this day, with some Messianic Jewish congregations holding meetings on both *Shabbat* and Sunday and commemorating both Jewish holidays and later Gentile Christian holidays, most notably Passover and Easter, or *Hanukkah* and Christmas.

There has been much confusion over the centuries about the possibility of Jews remaining Jewish yet being faithful disciples of Yeshua. Some Christians have thought that Jewishness is undesirable, associating it with legalism or dead traditions. Others have thought that an emphasis on Jewishness inevitably leads to a deemphasis of Yeshua. That's why we must say clearly today that Yeshua is at the center of our Jewishness. We don't want to move Him out of the center. We don't want to consider our Jewishness to be more important than Yeshua Himself.

In reality, the centrality of Yeshua and the emphasis on Jewishness are two different issues. It is possible to have a strong emphasis on Jewish identity and lifestyle, but no emphasis on Yeshua. This would be the case for rabbinic synagogues all over the world. It is also possible to have a strong emphasis on Jesus, but no emphasis on Jewish identity and lifestyle. This would be true of Gentile Christian churches all over the world. I believe that it is possible to have both a strong emphasis on Yeshua, placing Him at the center, and a strong emphasis on Jewishness. This is the case for Messianic Judaism.

Messianic Jews, Not Judaizers

Messianic Jewish synagogues are healthy when Yeshua is at the center and when there is a strong emphasis on Jewish lifestyle and identity.

Ray Pritz has documented that there were clear differences between the early Messianic Jews and the Judaizers in the first centuries after Yeshua. The Messianic Jews were often identified as *Nazarenes* in the first few centuries. In modern Israel, Christians are called *Notzrim,* a carry-over from this early Hebrew identification. The Nazarenes, like today's Messianic Jews, affirmed that Yeshua was the Messiah and that Jewish disciples should continue in their Jewish identity. But unlike the Judaizers, the Nazarenes did not believe that Gentiles had to convert to Judaism in order to faithfully follow Yeshua. While the Nazarenes would circumcise their own Jewish sons on the eighth day, the Judaizers would insist that Gentile converts must also be circumcised. The Nazarenes were also distinct theologically from the *Ebionites,* a sect that believed that Yeshua was the Messiah but did not accept that He was the fullness of God in bodily form.

Messianic believers understand that Yeshua is the Messiah and the God of Israel and of all the nations. We are convinced it is historically true that God came to the Jewish people in fullness and human form as Yeshua. We are convinced it is historically true that Yeshua was crucified by the Romans in Jerusalem and His death served as a redemptive sacrifice for our sins. We are convinced it is historically true that Yeshua was three days in the grave and then rose from the dead, appearing to His disciples in Jerusalem and in Galilee. We are convinced it is historically true that Yeshua ascended into the heavens, sending His Holy Spirit to dwell with all those who put their trust in Him. And we are convinced it will be historically true that Yeshua will return to Jerusalem as the long-awaited King Messiah.

We are persuaded that everyone who puts their trust in

Him will be redeemed and will have abundant life in this world and eternal life in the world to come. And we are persuaded that He forgives our sins and heals our sicknesses.

Because of all this, we are certain that it is appropriate to worship Yeshua and to serve Him with obedient joy. This understanding is central to Messianic Judaism. If you take Yeshua away from the center, you destroy Messianic Judaism. In our day, there are many different forms of Judaism. From the ultra-orthodox on one side, to the secular, humanistic Jews on the other side, each form of Judaism has certain distinctives. Sitting in many synagogues all over the world are Jews who are united in their appreciation for various traditions, but who nevertheless have widely different views about God and Messiah.

MY ARGUMENT FOR YESHUA AS MESSIAH

They say that when there are two Jews together, there are three opinions. As a people, we love to argue, sometimes just for the sake of argument. I think it was through my mother's father, Lou Poller, that I inherited the love of an argument. Don't get me wrong. I'm not talking about debate, or even reasoned discussion. I simply mean that my grandfather and I (often together) have enjoyed arguing about things that didn't matter at all. Once we expressed an opinion, we could defend it no matter how wrong we were. "Opinion before fact" could have been our watchword.

Well, this love for argument showed up in me in a funny way right after I had married. A friend was staying with us in our log cabin right after our honeymoon. I don't remember why, but our talk turned to Jesus. I have to admit I didn't know anything to speak of about Jesus, but I sure loved a good argument. When my friend Gene took his position, it was a little awkward for me. You see, he had been raised in an Episcopalian family. But he took the position that Jesus was not the Messiah. I don't know why he took that position

71

or what we might have possibly been talking about that could have led him to even make that point.

But I smelled a good argument in the air. Now this is the awkward part. I was raised in a Jewish family, and now I had to decide if I would try to win this particular argument. There was no way I could have won the argument by convincing either Gene or myself that Jesus really was the Messiah. But the lust for a good argument captivated me anyway. Plus I still thought there was a way to win.

"Gene, either Jesus is the Messiah, or He is not," I said. "It doesn't matter what you think. It's a matter of fact. If He is the Messiah, it doesn't matter if you say He's not. And if He's not the Messiah, it doesn't matter if you say that He is. Either He is or He isn't."

I was so proud of myself. There really wasn't anything Gene could say.

Messiah, as Personal Savior

Moses Maimonides, the great Jewish scholar who codified Jewish law, asserted that belief in Messiah was essential for every true Jew and a condition for eternal life. Yet in many synagogues and Jewish denominations, the belief in a personal Messiah has been replaced with the belief in a messianic age, brought about through good deeds, human progress, and perfection. And within many synagogues and Jewish denominations are members who do not believe that the God of Israel is real. They could be characterized in some cases as atheists, in other cases as agnostics. But there are vast numbers of Jews who have embraced a secularism that has its roots in the European Enlightenment and who have allowed it to strip God out of their Judaism.

Yet despite these differences, the most important distinctive for all Judaism is Yeshua Himself. There are different views about *halacha,* "Jewish law," about prayer, worship, and more. But the greatest difference is regarding Yeshua.

In our day, Jewish disciples are growing in number and

visibility. As we form Messianic congregations, we are again facing all the issues that the early disciples faced. What do we do with our own Jewishness; what do we do with our Jewish family, friends, and community; and what do we do with all the Gentiles with whom God is uniting us? But first and foremost, we must always ask, "What do we do with Yeshua?"

יהודים וגויים ביחד

JEWS AND GENTILES TOGETHER

······································

Love your neighbor as yourself.
—Leviticus 19:18

CHAPTER
FIVE

"WE ARE JEWS AND GENTILES TOGETHER IN ONE CONGREGATION."

"I've not heard of that," Anat Goldstein commented, her Israeli-accented English betraying no skepticism. We had rented Anat's apartment in a charming Jerusalem neighborhood for a holiday visit during *Sukkot,* the Feast of Tabernacles. Anat had a Ph.D. in counseling, and she worked in a clinic that was based on family systems theory. I was interested in her understandings and read several books from her library during our stay. But now she wanted to know more about us. I was trying to tell her that there were congregations in which both Jews and non-Jews worshiped.

I continued, "We worship together, and together we worship the God of Israel."

"So you don't worship the Christian God?" she asked.

"Actually, there are many Christians who understand that they serve the God of Israel," I responded.

"I've not heard of that," she repeated, now a little perplexed.

Her daughter, Deanna, joined the conversation. "What are the rules of your community?"

I wanted to make sense of her question, so I thought about her frame of reference. Every Jewish sect or splinter group has some rules or beliefs that differentiate and divide it from other Jewish groups.

Some groups are divided over their dress. One group

dresses like eighteenth-century Polish nobility. Others dress like their Yemenite forefathers. Some have long *payissin,* "earlocks;" some of these wrap the earlocks behind their ears, and others display them more prominently. The style of *kippah,* or "skullcap," one wears reveals something of his group identity. Some groups refuse to watch television or read secular newspapers.

Rules Yes, but Not Legalism

What are our rules? I wondered. I decided to use Yeshua's answer. He was asked a similar question: "Which is the greatest commandment in the Law?" (Matt. 22:36, NIV). A Pharisee wanted to know the first and foremost commandment. I've often noticed that many believers are uncomfortable with the question. Some think that any answer about commandments or rules will only be born of legalism or will ultimately lead to legalistic attitudes or behaviors. Yet Yeshua Himself did not shy away from the question. Nor did He dismiss it as irrelevant, as if the fullness of His New Covenant would render all of God's commandments irrelevant. Yeshua answered immediately and without hesitation.

Yeshua quoted the *Shema,* the definitive prayer of the Jewish people. Found in Deuteronomy 6:4, the *Shema* is the declaration of faith in the one true God. *Shema Yisrael Adonai Elohaynoo, Adonai Echad.* "Hear, O Israel: the LORD our God, the LORD is one" (NIV). Now this is not just a creed; it is a commandment, because it begins with an imperative calling us to listen; it implies that we will hearken in obedience. Yeshua continues with the following verse, known as the *Vehaftah. Vehaftah et Adonai Elohekha, b'khol l'vavkhah, oov'khol nafshakha, oov'khol m'odekha.* "Love the LORD your God with all your heart and with all your soul and with all your strength" (NIV).

Each day these same words are recited in Jewish synagogues all over the world. Taken carefully, they convey the essence of true Jewish faith. God desires to have a relationship with *people*. Religious behavior is one thing, but a loving relationship is another. First and foremost of all the *mitzvot*, "commandments," is the command to listen to God and to love Him with all of our being. True faith is unreserved. It is not confined to a place like a synagogue or a church or even the holy temple. It is neither relative nor privatized. It permeates; it possesses us entirely. This is because *faith* is a "relational" word, not a religious word. It speaks of trust and confidence, not merely ritual or all those things Abraham Joshua Heschel called "religious behaviorism."

Yeshua gives a good answer, but He doesn't stop. He adds, "There is a second commandment like the first: *Vehaftah l'rayakha kamokha.* You shall "love your neighbor as yourself" (NIV). Here Yeshua is quoting from Leviticus 19:18, a verse about love, in a context of grace and forgiveness in a book often regarded as filled with dry, dead ritualistic law. (See Matthew 22:39.)

The Book of Matthew recalls Yeshua's additional comment: "On these two commandments hang all the law (the *Torah)* and the Prophets (the *Nevi'im)."* While Marcion and others would discard the Old Testament from the Christian canon of Scripture, to Yeshua it was the repository of truth about Him, containing within it all the prophecies about Him and the wisdom that would lead people toward Him. One of His last acts, we're told in the final chapter of Luke, was to open the minds of His disciples so that they could understand the *Tanakh,* the Jewish Scriptures (Luke 24:45). At that point, these were the only Scriptures, because it would be years before the writings of the apostles would be completed and recognized as Scriptures too. Yeshua taught that the right interpretation of the *Tanakh* was based upon our understanding of the importance and priority of these first two commandments.

When I told Anat and her daughter that these two commandments were our guiding rules, I could observe their continued surprise. In their minds, Jews and Christians were completely separate. The twin concepts of the Jewish roots of Christianity and the Jewishness of Yeshua were foreign to them. That Yeshua would have spoken those words was unknown to them. That Gentiles would believe these words and join together with Jews was unthinkable.

The Mystery of Gentiles as Adopted Sons of Abraham

Paul wrote that this was a mystery long hidden, but in his time revealed. (See 1 Corinthians 2:7–10.) That God has given a place to the *Goyim,* "the Gentile nations," is still unknown to many Jewish people. Even more unbelievable is Paul's assertion that the Gentiles have been brought as adopted sons into the commonwealth of Israel.

For centuries, many Christians have turned this thought upside down, twisting away its true meaning. As a result, many Christians have come to think that they have replaced Israel and that the Jewish people have been set aside.

When the apostles first considered what to do with believing Gentiles, they accepted Peter's testimony about his experience in Caesarea, a provincial seat of Roman government and the place to which he had been summoned by Cornelius, a God-fearing Gentile. Like other God-fearers, Cornelius believed that the God of Israel was the one true God without converting to Judaism per se. Peter was explaining to those gathered in Cornelius' house how they could be saved by faith in Yeshua. While He was still instructing them, *HaRuach HaKodesh,* "the Holy Spirit," fell on those Gentiles, and they began to speak in unknown tongues. This reminds all of us who preach and teach that there is always more that could be said, but we should stop when the Holy Spirit has finished making His point.

Here were Gentiles, immersed in the Holy Spirit and speaking in unknown tongues! Now Peter's dream really made sense. Those unclean animals coming down in sheets—that was really about Gentiles, not food. God was making Gentiles clean through faith, and it happened right in front of Peter's eyes. As a result, he decided that Gentiles could be immersed in water in the name of Yeshua without converting to Judaism. In other words, Gentiles did not have to become Jews and enter into the Abrahamic covenant of circumcision.

The other apostles later agreed with Peter's decision and his reasoning. This understanding helped shape the apostolic pattern of evangelism: to the Jew first, and also to the Greek and Gentiles. The Greek-speaking world and, by implication, all nations were to be evangelized, not ignored. When Paul articulated this pattern—to the Jew first—he was not commenting on chronology but on priority. In every generation, the gospel must first be brought to the Jewish people. The gospel is not only relevant, it is *necessary* for the Jewish people.

Though some of their contemporaries insisted that there was no salvation without circumcision, this was rejected by the apostles. In this way, the Jewish apostles chose not to hinder the Gentiles who were turning to God. For the entire period covered by the New Testament writings, Jews remained Jews and non-Jews remained non-Jews, but they were united in congregations, in faith, in repentance, in immersion in water, in the laying on of hands, and in the Spirit.

Paul was circulating the Jerusalem Council's decision about Gentiles and circumcision to the congregations in the *Diaspora*. He took with him Timothy, the son of a Jewish mother and a Greek father. Though he had been taught the *Tanakh* from childhood by his believing Jewish grandmother, Eunice, Timothy had not been circumcised. This was not unusual, given that his parents were intermarried. But Paul reckoned Timothy Jewish, and he insisted that Timothy enter into Abraham's covenant through circumcision. The language of Acts 16:3 may even indicate that Paul himself circumcised Timothy. In any case, what is clear is that these first Jewish followers of Yeshua regarded themselves as Jewish and yet welcomed the non-Jews into their midst.

Thus began a chapter in one of the greatest sociological experiments of history, the bringing together of Jews and other nations into single congregations without insisting on the full assimilation of either.

These Jewish apostles went out to the nations, calling them with words that ignited repentance, faith, and immersion in the name of the Messiah of the Jews. They introduced the nations to the Jewish Scriptures and taught them how to worship and pray to the God of Israel. Sometimes we think of speaking in tongues as a Pentecostal or Charismatic Christian phenomenon. That makes it seem as if the Pentecostals taught everyone else about speaking in tongues. In fact, God used the early Messianic Jews to teach the nations about the baptism with the Holy Spirit.

For many Jews like Anat, Judaism and Christianity are historically and even eternally separate. But the humanity of Yeshua and the pattern of His disciples and apostles reveal the Jewishness of the trunk and root of the people of faith. Where once the first question was about Gentiles turning to Yeshua, the later question has become about Jews turning to Jesus.

The Jewish apostles rightly decided not to hinder the Gentiles who had received the gift of repentance that leads to life. But later, when Gentile Christians grew to outnumber Messianic Jews, they acted with less magnanimity. By A.D./C.E. 325, the Council of Nicea decided against the spirit of the Council of Jerusalem. Here this church council formally severed itself from the Jewishness of the root and trunk. Nicea would have no part of Jewishness. Like Antiochus Epiphanes and the Syrian-Greek Seleucids, the Nicean Council attempted to erase all Jewish distinctives from the body of Messiah. Circumcision of the sons of Jewish disciples was outlawed. So were the Jewish holidays, foremost among them both *Shabbat* and Passover. Congregational worship was formally transferred to Sunday, and Easter was calendarized so as not to coincide with Passover. Association with rabbinic Jews was banned, and

Jewish identity and lifestyle were made anathema.

THE SPIRIT OF AMALEK

The spirit of Amalek typifies all those who oppose the Jews and God's plan to use the Jews. This spirit has motivated many people under widely different circumstances, but always toward the same goal: the destruction of the Jewish people. (See Exodus 17:8–15; Numbers 24:20.) Sometimes the battle has been waged politically, sometimes militarily. Other times it is fought on the cultural front, or philosophically, or religiously. Pharaoh was motivated by the spirit of Amalek, as was Haman, and, of course, Hitler too—so motivated that he destroyed six million Jews on his way to the final solution.

In these days, as we put off all that Amalek has intended, we find that the church is putting off its anti-Semitism. Almost all of Israel's prophets understood that God in His faithfulness would judge Israel, but they almost all understood that His mercy would triumph over even His justice (James 2:13, NIV). They understood that God would use Gentile nations in judgment against the Jewish people. But the prophets always warned those nations that although they were instruments of judgment, they were not necessarily just. In the end, even prophets like the pessimist Jeremiah knew that God would restore the Jewish people, and woe to the nations that had been instruments of punishment or chastisement to the Jews.

Paul wrote the Ephesian community of believers that God's eternal plan to bring Jews and Gentiles together was now being revealed. (See Ephesians 3:1–5.) He said the part of *Torah* that produced enmity between Jews and Gentiles has now been overcome. The Gentiles are being received. It is this one body of Messiah, made up of Jews and Gentiles together, which is the *ecclessia* of Messiah. This is the body that displays God's wisdom to the realms of heaven, to angels and principalities alike. (See Colossians

2:15.) Ezekiel understood that a revived Israel is one key to world evangelism. (See Ezekiel 38:23.) When Israel is revived, the world will know that God Himself has done it.

Some wait for an eschatological conclusion, thinking that only then will God turn to the Jews. But we see for ourselves that God has already been pouring out His favor upon Zion. As Peter's theology was refined by the work of the Spirit, so is ours. Peter saw three thousand Jewish people repent in one day. As Joel had prophesied, this pouring out of the Spirit meant that there would be dreams and visions from God, and Peter received both. As Joel had said, the Spirit would be poured out on all flesh and blood. As again we see thousands of Jewish people repenting, we must adjust our theological boundaries to understand that this *again* is a day of the Lord's visitation, a day of His visiting the Jewish people.

From Israel's earliest history, God has been using non-Jews to build up the Jewish people. If Amalek is the picture of all those who oppose the Jews and God's plan to use the Jews, then who is the picture of the people who choose to stand with the Jews and with God's plan for the Jewish people?

RUTH: A MODEL FOR GENTILE CHRISTIANS

I believe that Ruth is the perfect example for Gentile Christians. Ruth was a Moabitess, a descendant of the incestuous relationship between Lot and one of his daughters. The name *Moab* even means "from father," a haunting reminder of the tribe's ignoble origin.

Yet Ruth joined herself with the Jewish people, not converting to Judaism as some Orthodox Jews argue, but following that earlier pattern of the faith of the patriarchs. In a family of widows, the Moabitess Ruth said to her Jewish mother-in-law, Naomi: "Where you go I will go, and where you stay I will stay. Your people will be my people and your God my God" (Ruth 1:16, NIV).

Abraham and his descendants were promised people-hood, a covenant relationship with God, and a land. Ruth chose the people, the God, and the land of the Jewish people. In this way she chose a Jewish destiny, redirecting her life onto the same path that would take the Jewish people to their destination in God. Like Abraham, she left her people, her god, and her land, and she went to a land she knew not. There in Israel she was lifted up from her poverty and vulnerability through the kindness of a kinsman-redeemer. With Boaz, Ruth gave birth to Obed, father of Jesse, whose youngest son was David who became Israel's king and the one to whom was given a promise that his descendant would be Israel's Messiah.

This faithful woman from the unclean tribe of Moab saw the fulfillment to her Jewish friends' prophetic prayer and blessing: "May you be like Rachel and Leah, the two who built the house of Israel." (See Ruth 4:11.)

MESSIANIC JUDAISM DISTINCTIVES

One of the questions I have been asked regularly is, "What is Messianic Judaism?"

For many people, this idea of a Messianic Jewish congregation is brand new. Of course, we declare that we Messianic Jews are Jews and that we have our congregations. But some voices say we're not really Jews. You can look at our faces and know that is not true. So who are we and what are we about?

Messianic Judaism is made of Jews and non-Jews who believe that Yeshua is the promised Messiah and who want to worship in congregations that promote Jewish lifestyle and identity. We are a movement that is being used by God to restore the Jewish people. And God is using us powerfully.

Some people say, "This is a very new thing."

I say, "Not really."

Reporters often ask, "When did your movement start?"

The answer is, "Two thousand years ago in Jerusalem."

Now this is important to know because we are one of the oldest forms of faith in the Jewish community. Our headquarters was based in Jerusalem. All the original founders of this movement were Jewish. We go back two thousand years to the Jewish homeland.

Most of the popular branches of Judaism today are much younger. Progressive, or Reform Judaism, has roots that are about one hundred years old. Reconstructionist Judaism is even newer.

What many people think of as true, authentic Judaism is, in fact, relatively new. For instance, the Hasidic Judaism started in the eighteenth century in Ukraine, and so, in a sense, we are their older brothers. But they don't know that.

Though the *Chabad* are considered by many today to be "expert Jews" because of their ultra-Orthodoxy and prominent outreaches to unaffiliated Jews, they were originally considered by other Orthodox Jews to be a dangerous sect.

Despite opposition that comes from many rabbinic corners, it is important for us to know we have standing before God. We are an important part of the Jewish community. We are called by God with a purpose. We are called to make a simple declaration: The promised Messiah for Israel is Yeshua, and the most Jewish thing we can do is put our trust in Him. We don't become less Jewish when we do this; we become *more* Jewish.

Everyone who is called to be part of a Messianic Jewish congregation has gifts from the Holy Spirit. Everyone called to the Messianic movement has vision and revelation from God. There is a calling on our lives, and what we do will make a profound difference.

We must volunteer freely because this is the hallmark of the day of the Lord's power. Together we must serve the Lord. This requires that we make a commitment to our Messianic congregation. It's time to stop being just a visitor. It's time to "stop dating and get married."

What makes Messianic Judaism different from other forms of Judaism?

First, we are centered on Yeshua. Yeshua is at the very center of the life of every Messianic Jew. If you move Him out of the center, you destroy the Messianic Jewish way of life. Only when our eyes are fixed on Him can we see the rest of our Jewishness clearly. All of our Jewishness is brought into focus by our understanding of who Yeshua is and how we are to relate to Him as Lord and Savior.

We understand that Yeshua is the Messiah, the God of Israel and of all the nations. He died as a sacrifice for our sins. He became the sacrifice for our sin, even though He had no sin. In this way, He has transferred to us the righteousness of God.

He was dead for three days, and then He rose from the grave. He appeared to His disciples in Jerusalem and Galilee, then He ascended into heaven. In His last words, He instructed His Jewish disciples to make disciples of all the nations, because this is the call of the Jewish people—to be a light to the nations. He sent His Holy Spirit, and He will return to Jerusalem as King Mashiach.

So we look for Him, and we wait for Him. He heals us of our sicknesses and our diseases. And we worship Him. Everyone who puts their trust in Yeshua will be saved from their sins, will have their sins forgiven, and will have abundant life in this world and eternal life in the world to come.

YESHUA AT THE CENTER

Our Jewish identity is incomplete without knowing who Yeshua is. Only when we have made Him the very center of our lives can the rest of our Jewishness take on its eternal purposes.

In August 1997 when we were holding the International Festival of Jewish Music and Dance in Riga, I met a woman in her seventies. She told me she was an obstetrician and midwife. Along with thousands of others that evening, she had come to one of the largest auditoriums in the capital of Latvia to listen to Messianic Jewish music, to watch Messianic

Jewish dance, and to hear Messianic Rabbi Jonathan Bernis share the Good News of Messiah Yeshua.

She was clearly intelligent and happy to be at the festival. Nevertheless I could tell something was on her mind. She asked me this question, "Why doesn't our rabbi, our *rebbe,* want us to come to the festival?" She was at the festival, so she obviously wasn't obeying the rabbi's wishes. She was so typical of our Jewish people, intelligent, pensive, and independent.

I answered her, "The rabbi doesn't want you to make up your mind for yourself about Yeshua. He's afraid that if you come here, you will become convinced that Yeshua is in fact the Jewish Messiah, and you will become a Messianic Jew like us."

And she responded, "I already believe that Yeshua is the Messiah!"

I thought aloud, "I bet your rabbi doesn't know that."

Having overseen thousands of births, she testified to me about God. "How could anyone *not* believe there is a God? Not once have I had a child die during childbirth. Not once has a mother died. I have never made a mistake in childbirth. This is not because of me. It is only because of God's help. Of course, Yeshua is the Messiah—I have known this for many years!"

Like so many Jews throughout the world, here was another wise professional, a *babushke,* a "grandmother" who had discovered for herself that the Jewish Messiah had come. Intent on preserving her Jewish identity, she remained in the rabbinic synagogue, quietly worshiping Yeshua for all these years. All over the world we find such Jews. Faithful to Yeshua and to their Jewishness, they have been praying and waiting for a Messianic synagogue.

She was delighted with our invitation for her to come to the Messianic synagogue in Riga. Less than a year old, the Messianic synagogue had been prepared to receive many new Jewish believers from the festival. What joy I felt when I saw her at the next two services at the Messianic congregation. Together with her husband, she had come to every concert of the festival. Now she was finding her place in a Messianic Jewish synagogue, a place where Jews could freely worship together as Jews, happily giving praise to Yeshua the Messiah, keeping Him at the center.

LESSONS FROM A JEWISH NUN

Edith Stein is a good example of one who kept Yeshua at the center. She was raised in a very religious Jewish family in Germany. She not only converted to Catholicism; she became a nun. Despite the difficulties of family and community misunderstandings or prejudices, she held on to her Jewish identity until her death.

Stein had sought refuge in Holland, but even there Jews were being rounded up and taken to concentration camps. Though Dutch pastors protested and many Dutch chose to put on the yellow star-of-David armband that the Nazis forced the Jews to wear, the Germans were steadfast in their plan to eradicate the Jews from all the earth.

The Bishop of Utrect sent a telegram, which was read in all the Dutch Catholic parishes on July 26, 1942. It read:

> Dear Brethren:
>
> When Jesus drew near to Jerusalem and saw the city before Him, He wept over it and said, "O, if even today you understood the things that make for peace! But now they are concealed from your sight." . . . Dear brethren, let us begin by examining ourselves in a spirit of profound humility and sorrow. Are we not partly to blame for the calamities that we are suffering? Have we always sought first for God's kingdom and His righteousness? Have we always fulfilled the demands of justice and charity toward our fellowmen? . . . When we examine ourselves, we are forced to admit that all of us have failed . . . Let us beseech God . . . to bring about swiftly a just peace in

the world and to strengthen the people of Israel so sorely tested in these days, leading them to true redemption in Christ Jesus.

A week later, all Jewish Catholics in Holland were arrested. Edith, with her sister Rosa, approached a German squad car. "Come, Rosa," she said, "We're going for our people."

Her friend, Father Johannes Hirschmann, would later say:

> Edith Stein learned to unite intimately her historically determined cross of membership in the Jewish people with the cross of Jesus Christ. She became convinced that as a Jew she was being called to share in her people's sufferings, and she solemnly committed herself before God not to let her vows or baptism give the slightest advantage over the most wretched of her persecuted people. . . .
>
> I will never forget the conversations I had with this genuinely Christian philosopher when time and time again she would insist that hatred must never be given the last word . . . Hadn't Jesus, when He prayed for those who hated Him, those who crucified and pierced Him, turned His wounds into the symbol of love that proved to be stronger in the end?
>
> There is no question that Auschwitz will always remain for us as a terrifying revelation of the destructive potential of human lovelessness. But there is another revelation at Auschwitz, infinitely transcending the first: The love that endures the cross ultimately overcomes all lovelessness. This is the love that says to the cross: "For the sake of the love that has come to men through Jesus' cross and wounds, I love you and I testify—*hate is not stronger than love!*" [1]

Chutzpah!

One night outside the festival auditorium in Riga, I met

another Jewish woman who said that she loves to sing the songs of the Jewish people. She had some advice for us about how we should sing an old Jewish song, "Yiddishe Mama." I asked her to sing, and she performed it the way she thought it should be sung. With the passion of her elderly vibratto, she sang it all the way through in perfect *Yiddish,* ending with a theatrical gesture and a short bow.

Playfully I said, "Maybe we'll have *you* sing at the festival!" I was preparing to share with her about Yeshua, but before I could she spoke up.

She smiled and said, "I'm part of a choral group in the synagogue in a nearby city, but I also come to the Messianic congregation in Riga when I can."

She told me that when her rabbi found out, he said, "You can't sing in our choir and believe in Jesus."

This short, spunky Jewish *babushke* folded her arms as she relived the moment, and recounted her defiant response. Her brow furrowed, her eyes began to burn, her face dramatically expressing *chutzpah,* that unmovable Jewish boldness, which is difficult to define but impossible to ignore.

She told the rabbi, "I have been part of the choral group, and I will be part of the choral group." Only a *Yiddishe* mama can do this. She looked at me intently, her eyes almost two feet below mine, staring. I tried to imagine the rabbi's response when she insisted, " I will go to this synagogue, and I will go to the Messianic synagogue." And then she began to preach. "No one can tell me that I cannot believe in Yeshua!"

We Jews can be independent, even defiant. Sometimes it serves us well. And sometimes it causes much *tsuris,* "heartache." This time, it was causing one rabbi *tsuris,* but for another, for me, it brought great joy.

דייגים וצייידים

FISHERS AND HUNTERS

· ·

*Behold, I will send for many fishers, saith the LORD, and
they shall fish them; and after will I send for many hunters,
and they shall hunt them from every mountain, and from
every hill, and out of the holes of the rocks. For mine eyes
are upon all their ways: they are not hid from my face,
neither is their iniquity hid from mine eyes.*
—JEREMIAH 16:16–17

CHAPTER
SIX

LET ME TELL YOU ABOUT MY APOCALYPTIC DREAM. SANDY AND I WERE on the road to Jerusalem in war-ravaged times. I was afraid, but Sandy—who had the necessary discernment—was not. She saw into the darkness and brought me peace. . . .

"WE'RE GOING TO JERUSALEM!"

Besides those dreams in which I can fly or step and glide like a man on the moon, my most memorable dreams are almost always apocalyptic. Something has gone wrong in the world in each of these dreams, and the present peace and relative calm in my part of the world have given way to fearful circumstances and instability. I have such dreams periodically. I wake up from these dreams with a sense of foreboding. Thinking back, stirring my memories, I recall vivid details and often wonder about the prophetic significance of the dream. It's not that every dream has meaning, of course, but many more dreams do than we typically think.

This one dream—Sandy and me, on the road to Jerusalem, in the midst of war—was so powerful, so alarming, so pregnant with implication that I realized even while I slept that I must remember the dream, understand it, and tell Sandy about it.

The geography was familiar, clearly America, though not identifiable. Sandy and I were walking, intent on keeping to ourselves in this strange circumstance. We needed some-where to sleep, so we began to enter houses, looking for a suitable place to spend the night. As we looked inside one house, we saw the signs of abandonment. The dining-room table was set, but a thin layer of dust had settled on every-thing, diminishing the table's sheen. This layer of dust was the common clue in all the homes we entered as to how long it had been since the family of a home had left. In the first home, it looked as if they had left a month or so earlier.

In this dream, I didn't have memories of what had caused the abandonment of so many neighborhoods and houses, but as I experienced the dream, I began to understand. There must have been a war—either recently or expected—and throughout this particular territory, residents and homeowners had left hurriedly. There was no sign that people had gathered up their valuables or carefully pre-pared these houses for their absence. Rather, it looked as if people had been suddenly removed, no evidence of packing, no visible evidence of violence or trauma.

But in this house, on one corner of a round table was a knapsack, obviously newly placed. Betrayed by the contin-uous fine layer of dust underneath it, the knapsack drew our attention. We noticed some clothes laid out on the fur-niture and instinctively understood that someone had arrived just before us, with the same intentions.

At this point, I realized that the city was not entirely aban-doned. From what we could see, it was no longer inhabited. But, there were people like us, passing through, coming from somewhere, perhaps going anywhere. Quiet, keeping to ourselves, engaging no one, this was the way we should carry ourselves. Don't stand out in any way, avoid drawing attention to ourselves. Anonymity at any cost.

When I saw the knapsack, I turned around and began to walk out of the house. We were all squatters, and whoever arrived first had full rights to the house. No one stayed for long, because we were all on our way out. I thought about the danger. Whoever that knapsack belonged to could be threatened by us and react with hostility. After all, there was a war going on somewhere, and who could tell a friend from a dangerous enemy? So I hurried to leave, but Sandy didn't follow.

Before I could impress upon her the necessity and wisdom of leaving quickly, the knapsack's owner appeared in the foyer. I would have left silently, but Sandy spoke to him.

"Where are you headed?" she asked. "We're going to Jerusalem."

I was afraid, troubled that Sandy was not only talking to a stranger, but she was also speaking about our plans. This was not wise, and it could prove dangerous. How could she know this stranger's attitudes? What if he hated us for the simple reason of our destination?

To my surprise, he said that he also was headed toward Jerusalem. "May I go with you?" he asked.

Before I could take in his answer and Sandy's response, adrenaline rushed through my sleeping body, waking me up. It was then that I heard that voice, the Holy Spirit's voice, telling me to remember this dream and to speak to Sandy about it.

As I considered the dream's meaning, I realized that it wasn't primarily about a desperate future period. It was about Jerusalem, Israel, destiny, and Sandy and me.

Rabbi Joseph Soloveitchik points out that the Jewish people are a people with a destiny. That means we are headed toward a destination. The meaning of our lives is only discerned as we realize what that destination would be. Life takes on a new significance, and all the various parts of our daily existence can become aligned when we realize how all the fragments are brought together by the vision and destination God has placed in our hearts and minds. We are not vagabonds or nomads, but rather people on a journey—a perilous one, perhaps, but our destination is our purpose. We are sojourners, aliens, not citizens of this common land, but looking toward a full citizenship in a coming realm and age.

What I perceived in my dream as wisdom was really fear and self-protection. This contributed to my discomfort with Sandy's openness. As I woke up, I realized that the Lord wanted me to understand that we were truly on our way to Jerusalem and that Sandy, far more than I, was alert to that reality and able to spot those people who were headed toward the same destination.

This one man I saw as unimportant—and potentially a danger—Sandy realized was a fellow pilgrim, ready to travel together.

A People of Destiny

Since that dream, we have met several people who either did not impress me or to whom I did not respond with any kind of interest. But Sandy saw something in them, far beyond what I could see. She and Chantal Winograd would take a special assignment at some of our first Hear O Israel festivals. When the concert halls would become too crowded, we would have to close the front doors, consolidate everyone inside, and look for empty seats. Sandy and Chantal would look for Jewish people and make sure they got in the back door of the concert hall.

In Minsk, Belarus, in August 1994, we had thousands more come to the festival than we had room for. Russian news media reported that there were more than twenty thousand turned away, but we estimated between five and ten thousand. The crush of humanity was so great that the local police closed the entrances and would not allow another soul into the hall. Outside were thousands of disappointed people and a few of our team members. Our team began to talk to the people who were unable to get inside, sharing the gospel and engaging them in dialogue. But there were a few moments when the crowd was too forceful, and the police responded in kind. People pushed forward, trying to get into the closed facility. And the police pushed back. *Babushkas* and children were caught in the middle, and some cried out in pain.

The next night we wanted to see a greater calm and control at the front doors. With the help of the police force, we set up barricades, channels that we could open and close, allowing people in, or keeping them out. The commander loaned me his bullhorn, and with my interpreter's help, I asked the crowd to be peaceful and kind. In essence, he gave command of his troops to me and authorized me to address the situation. When I look at pictures from that night, my efforts seemed preposterous.

"Stop pushing," I urged this crowd of thousands, asking them to be nice to each other. Miraculously the crowd came under control. Slowly we let people in whenever we discovered yet another seat.

While I was guarding the front door, making sure that every seat was filled, Sandy was finding people and bringing them in through the back door. Once Sandy found a woman who was crying. She knew she needed to get her in. With her, it turned out, were a handful of friends and relatives who had come from hours away, had not been able to get in the night before, and couldn't come back the next night. With Richard Glickstein, Sandy organized a little operation to sneak them through the crowd at the back door and get them in. What Sandy thought was discreet was understood by quite a few people. By the time she got this little group to the back door area, she realized that the crowd at the back door should also be brought in. Sandy found a way to get all of them in that night. And she and Chantal later found more. Sometimes our efforts are like this: We go after *one* person, but we end up with dozens.

This became Sandy and Chantal's special mission: Find the Jewish people who had not been able to get in through the front and get them in the back door. It took planning, quick wits, a lot of cooperation, but most of all *discernment*.

God is stirring people's hearts in this hour, and all we sometimes need to do is recognize those who have been stirred and bring them in. In King Cyrus' day, God wanted the Jewish people to return to Jerusalem and to Him. The Lord stirred their spirits, brought in leadership, and provided material resources. The city was rebuilt and the people learned again to walk with the Lord. The *Torah* was reclaimed, praise and worship were restored, gift ministries were renewed, the people learned to minister cooperatively, and the celebration of the holidays was restored. Ungodly influences were routed, and prayer with fasting and intercession returned. (See the Book of Ezra.)

JERUSALEM IN PEOPLE'S HEARTS

God is putting Jerusalem in people's hearts. Christians are praying for the peace of Jerusalem, for her integrity, unity, and revival. And God is putting the Jewish people in the hearts of Christians too.

I went to the former Soviet Union in February 1993 for the first time. Jonathan Bernis and Bob Weiner organized a special conference in Moscow for Jewish believers. Some seven hundred people came to this important event.

I taught two classes on subjects that were dear to my heart. The first was about home groups and how to incorporate Jewish elements into small groups. I recited the *Shema,* the foremost prayer of the Jewish people. A holy hush came over the group, and I watched as Jewish people were being stirred. Slowly I repeated the *Shema,* and everyone wrote it down and transliterated it into Russian letters for their future use. I can't really explain it, but I recognize that the restoration of Jewishness brings life to Jewish believers. Somehow God uses the *Shema* to stir up the Jewish soul.

I think of the closing remarks of Dr. Viktor Frankl, in his classic work about surviving the Holocaust, *Man's Search for Meaning:*

Our generation is realistic, for we have come to know

man as he really is. After all, man is that being who invented the gas chambers of Auschwitz; however, he is also that being who entered those gas chambers upright, with the Lord's Prayer or the *Shema Yisrael* on his lips.[1]

In an important way, Jewishness is part of the root and trunk of faith. It was the faith of the Jewish patriarchs that is our pattern as believers. It was the faith of the Jewish prophets that has laid hold of our hearts. Of course, Yeshua is the vine, and we are all branches who draw our life from him. But he came as a Jew, to the Jewish people, and when Jewish people discover Yeshua and Jewishness together, their lives are enlarged, as is their faith.

The second class I taught in Moscow was about anti-Semitism. We talked about two very different kinds of anti-Semitism. The first is universally recognized as detestable, having a satanic source. The Nazi's anti-Semitism was of this kind. The second is subtler, because it is couched in Christian terminology. When Christians express hatred for the Jewish people, it is incredibly disheartening for Jewish believers. Whether it is intentional or not, and whether or not it is rooted in replacement theology, the effect on Jewish people is similar: Jews learn to hide their Jewishness, and they learn to keep themselves separate.

The remedy, I believe, is genuine love from Christians to the Jews. When that love is expressed practically and honorably, it has a healing effect on Jewish people.

BUILDING TOGETHER

It is not our job to call people to the Messianic movement, merely to vocalize the call. It is God Himself who actually calls someone, and He is the one who stirs up their spirits. (See Ezra 1.) Knowing this, we go into cities looking for those who are already called and sharing with them in a way that enables them to respond to the call. It's much easier this way and brings much less heartache. We want to work with those who are called and responsive, because we can build with them.

In June 1997 we helped plant a new Messianic congregation in Zhitomir, Ukraine. With the help of Pastor Vasile, we had a special meeting for Jewish members of his church. Sandy and I led a team to give a "taste of Messianic Judaism" to these Jewish (and non-Jewish) believers. The worship team from the Messianic Jewish Bible Institute in Odessa was with us, along with various leaders from our other congregations in the former Soviet Union. I explained the Messianic vision; then we had a time of Messianic praise, worship, and dance. When the MJBI worship team sang the *Shema,* the presence of the Lord was so anointed that people began to weep. The *Shema* is a call to the Jewish people to hear and hearken, and God used it to awaken the long-dormant identities of so many Jewish people in the meeting.

With dancers from our other congregations leading the way, that first Zhitomir meeting in June turned into a huge *hora. Shalom* and joy are best friends, and when both touch people's hearts, the people are stirred to action. And nothing produces or expresses Jewish joy like Messianic Jewish dancing. After the dance, we had a time of ministry to the people from Zhitomir who felt God calling them to help build the brand-new congregation. Prophetic ministry and intercession were powerful over these people, and a leadership core was formed in a moment.

Pastor Vasile offered use of his church building for the new congregation. At the first *Shabbat* service, I explained that there were Christians like Pastor Vasile who love Jewish people. Because of their generosity, we had a free place to meet. I felt it was important to share that publicly, because there were some in the city who didn't want us to meet in a church building because of their opinion that all Jews are afraid of Christians and Christianity. It is true that Christianity has disappointed the Jewish people, most notably by not standing up for the Jews during our tribulation in the Holocaust, and also for promoting at times an anti-Jewish sentiment. Rather than avoid that history, I think it is good to confront it. But best of all is to *replace* it. When Christian leaders like Pastor Vasile stand with the Jewish people and help us as we establish Messianic congregations, it is a great encouragement. Some of the key leaders from Pastor Vasile's church were Jews, and he encouraged them to follow God's prompting if they felt they should become part of the new Messianic congregation.

"HE UNDERSTANDS . . . "

Right before this first Zhitomir *Shabbat* service began, I noticed that there were many elderly Jewish people present, all of an age that meant they had survived the Holocaust. I approached one of these Jewish women with an evangelistic intent. I asked her if she had heard of Yeshua. "Yes," she answered, "and I love Him." She told me her story, how she had been taken as a child to one of the Nazis' mass execution sites. Though the machine guns fired, she wasn't hit, and she was pushed into the mass grave. For the rest of the day, bodies fell upon her, yet she lay quietly among the dead and dying. Under the cover of night, she crawled out of the pit and was taken in by a Gentile family.

Her eyes filled with tears as she repeated, "I love Yeshua. He's the only one who understands. He was also covered with blood."

Thousands of years ago the prophet Jeremiah wrote that there was coming a time when fishers, then hunters would come for the Jewish people. In the late nineteenth century and early twentieth century, Zionists went throughout Russia and Eastern and Western Europe, saying that it was time for the Jewish people to return to the land of Israel. These Zionists were the fishers. The hunters came before that generation had ended.

When I spoke to that Moscow class on anti-Semitism, I was overwhelmed with the seriousness of the historic moment in which we now live. The Jews survived the

Nazis; the hunters did not destroy us. Israel was reestablished, and the modern Messianic movement has been given life. Yet there is coming another cycle, I am afraid, of fishers and hunters. We, the Messianic Jews, are today's fishers, calling the Jewish people back to God and back to the land of promise. Coming later, perhaps within this generation, will again be the hunters.

We mustn't forget this. By nature I am optimistic, though admittedly my dreams have an apocalyptic bent. Despite the season of openness we are now in to the gospel, we can't remain overly optimistic about the future. *The hunters will come again.* We must be ready.

While it is still day, we must give ourselves to the restoration of the Jewish people, to the recovery of lost Jewish identities, and to the restoration of the place of Yeshua as the Messiah of the Jewish people.

I have had the privilege of seeing thousands of Jewish people turn to Yeshua through the anointed ministry of Jonathan Bernis, the founder of Hear O Israel Ministries. And I have also seen many come to faith through the ministries of many of our colaborers who have shared the gospel one-on-one on the streets of the former Soviet Union, in the homes of the Jewish people who live there, and at the meetings of the Messianic congregations that have been planted.

I have also had the privilege of making friends with some anointed Christian pastors, whose love for the Jewish people is profound and well-established. What a joy to see God use them to reach our people with the message of Yeshua, and to see God use them to help establish new Messianic congregations for the Jewish believers. In a world filled with selfishness and disinterest for the needs of others, it encourages me constantly to think about those pastors who have chosen to stand with our people. When trouble comes again to the former Soviet Union, men and women like this will receive an extra portion of trouble. First, they will be persecuted for being Christians. Second, they will be persecuted for helping the Jews. Lord, give grace and strength to these mighty men and women of God as they choose to take up their positions with You and the Jewish people.

BEYOND HELP AND HUMANITARIANISM

Peter Serachenko is the Pentecostal bishop of the Odessa, Ukraine, region. With his help, we have been able to hold our largest festival, drawing over sixty thousand people to three nights of concerts. He has also helped us get our Bible school started, helped with the Messianic congregation we have planted, and helped with humanitarian aide programs organized by the leaders of the Gateways to Zion Messianic congregation, David and Leslye Schneier. When we first met, I asked Bishop Peter why he loved the Jewish people and why he was helping us.

Bishop Peter told me that he grew up in a large, poor family. He recalled the shame and disrespect he felt from the other children at school. Only one boy treated him with dignity. That boy was a Jew. Peter grew up in the Pentecostal movement, became a respected pastor, and then became a bishop. The other boy grew up and became the mayor of Odessa. Together they have cooperated on various humanitarian projects to help Jews, Christians, and others in their city.

Pastor Nikolai is the "second" pastor of Word of Truth Church in Riga, Latvia. After our festival in Riga in August 1997, we needed a meeting place for the growing Messianic congregation. Pastor Nikolai offered his building to Samuel Cipen, the leader of the Messianic synagogue. At the first meeting following the festival, Pastor Nikolai shared how he came to love the Jewish people. He said it must have come from his mother's milk. His parents were "righteous Gentiles," Christians who had hidden the Jews from the Nazis. Helping the Jews, even at their own peril, was his family's legacy.

A holy hush came upon the group as we listened to Pastor Nikolai assert that the free sharing of the building was simply a reflection of his family's love and devotion to the Jewish people.

Pastor Nikolai grew up in a conservative Pentecostal family. His mother's parents lived in the village of Grichinovivichi, in a largely Jewish area, the Gomel region of Belarus. During the time of the Nazi occupation of Belarus, his grandfather, Vasile Korzh, hid about twenty-five Jews on his farm. The only place large enough to hide them was a "swinehouse," the muddy, filthy shed where the pigs were raised. For two or three weeks, these Jews hid from the Germans. Then Korzh determined that it would not be safe for them any longer. He came up with a plan to evacuate the Jews one by one.

The peril was great. The Jews had to get to the forest in order to escape to real safety. But to get there, they must pass a Nazi outpost. Vasile Korzh devised a simple plan: He would hand-carry each Jewish man, woman, and child, one by one in a heavy burlap sack. Carefully he instructed each of his charges not to move or make a sound. Once a person was safely hidden in the bag, he hoisted the heavy sack, with the neck of the sack tied closed with a rope and hanging over his shoulder.

"Where are you going?" the Nazis would ask.

"To the forest," he would answer.

"And what is in the sack?" the inquiry would continue.

"Just one of my dead swine. I will take it to the people who live in the forest, and they will bury it so that it will not rot and contaminate my well."

"Very well—then go on."

This simple deception worked again and again, and finally Korzh was known as the man with too many dead swine.

Isaiah had prophesied that God would turn His attention with miracles to the Gentiles, and they would "bring your sons in their arms and carry your daughters on their shoulders. Kings will be your foster fathers, and their queens your nursing mothers" (Isa. 49:22–23, NIV).

Perhaps this ancient prophecy was tumbling through the minds of the Jews as one brave soul carried so many of them upon his shoulders in humble sacks.

Once they arrived in the forest, Korzh would take each Jew to an underground hiding place. The partisans had created these subterranean fortresses—out of sight, out of mind. *Better that no one else knows,* they all thought. And so the ten Jewish families made it out of the village safely, into the forest, and thus into the hands of those who were fighting for their freedom. Each day, Korzh's wife would carry a basket of food into the forest, there to nourish the Jews who had grown familiar with, though never accustomed to, the daily hunger.

After the final Jew had been taken into the forest, someone reported to the Nazis that Korzh was a traitor and was hiding Jews. Nazi troops came to his farm, dominated the area around the swinehouse, and then fired upon it relentlessly until not an inhabitant was left alive. They thought they were firing upon Jews, but alas, it was only the swine who had perished.

When the soldiers discovered there were no Jews, they were outraged. They tied up Vasile Korzh, binding him in rope, tying his wrists together, then dragging him behind a horse. Horribly he was dragged, with such force that the rope from the horse to his wrists pulled tight and powerfully, snapping Korzh's wrist, pulling it out of the socket, then finally ripping off his hand. Blood flowed forcefully as the driven horse continued to drag its victim. Finally they stopped, left Korzh for dead, and went on their way.

Yet someone came to help, carried his near-lifeless body into the forest, bringing this simple hero into a hidden Soviet Army hospital camp. His hand forever gone, the medical unit was able to sew up what was left of his arm and stabilize him. Nikolai's grandmother fled into the forest, and the Nazis burned the farm and the swinehouse to the ground.

The family joined the partisans, and remained in the cover of the forests until the war concluded. Korzh's brother, a general in the Soviet Army, helped them and the partisans.

"For all this," Pastor Nikolai says, "my family has received a very big blessing. It is good to bless the Jews," he says. "Since we began blessing the Messianic congregation, we have been blessed. Our church has grown in a few months from four hundred to almost eight hundred people. And our tithes and offerings have doubled. Every time we give to the Messianic Jews, we receive a greater blessing."

His testimony makes real God's promise to bless those who bless Abraham.

Pastor Nikolai also told me that the Messianic festival in Riga was the first event that brought Christians together from every denomination and background. Somehow, all the believers were able to set aside their differences, to join together with the Jewish people. What a remarkable testimony that an event, intended to reach Jewish people first, was also successful in helping Christians find unity. This, I think, reveals something of the power that comes from taking the gospel to "the Jew first, and also to the Greek and the Gentile." We, the fishers, must prepare a people to survive when hunters come the next time.

היהודים הנסתרים

THE HIDDEN JEWS

•••

Wear the Yellow Badge with pride.
— ROBERT WELTSCH, APRIL 1933

CHAPTER
SEVEN

MADELEINE ALBRIGHT WAS RAISED A CATHOLIC, AS AN ADULT SHIFTED to the Episcopal Church, and during the course of her confirmation in 1997 as United States secretary of state discovered that her parents were Jewish. This discovery of Jewishness was treated with suspicion by many in the Jewish world who thought Albright had either deceived herself or refused to regard information about her Jewish background, which she had known about for years. Her motives, the critics claimed, were shame and embarrassment, and she sought to protect herself from this unwelcome fact of her Jewishness. Thus she was just one more Jew who had, for all intents, converted out in order to live in a Gentile world without stigma.

Whatever Albright's true motivations may have been, her situation is not so unusual. Throughout the world are the descendants of Jewish people who have been raised as non-Jews. I think of them as the *hidden Jews.* The vast majority were raised as non-Jews because of *halacha,* Orthodox Jewish law, which regards as Jews only those people whose mother is Jewish. With the increasing incidence of intermarriage, there is a growing number of people with Jewish ancestry who are not considered Jews.

Let's take the case of a Jewish family, with four children, two boys and two girls. If they all grow up and marry Gentiles, then the boys—now men—would not produce any Jewish children. However, the girls—now women—would have only Jewish children. So in this particular situation, with four intermarried couples, only two of the families would have Jewish children according to *halacha*.

Repeat this into the next generation, and the math is easy to understand. With only half of that generation qualifying as Jews, then we are now down to one-fourth of the total families having *halachically* Jewish children.

So it is the *halachic* Orthodox Jewish world that defines this outcome. No wonder intermarriage leads to a non-Jewish identity! This is a consequence of Orthodox rules. Reform Judaism rejects a strict rule of matrilineal descent and, like Messianic Judaism, considers Jewish anyone who has either a father or a mother who is Jewish. After all, Abraham married a non-Jew, as did his son Isaac, his grandson Jacob, and his great-grandson Joseph. Jacob, whose name was changed to Israel, elevated Joseph's sons, Manasseh and Ephraim, from the status of grandsons to the full status of sons even though their mothers were not Jewish. Moses married a non-Jew, yet God insisted that his son be circumcised according to the covenant made with Abraham and counted among the Jewish people, though he was not given any priestly or authoritative role. Nevertheless, it remains that the patriarchs and Moshe Rabbeinu, Moses, our great teacher and rabbi, married non-Jews although their children were reckoned among the nation of Israel.

Ruth the Moabitess, was not a Jewess, yet she was the great-grandmother of King David, and her children, grandchildren, great-grandchildren, and beyond were counted among the Jews. To David was given the promise of a descendant who would be the Messiah of the Jewish people. The apostles record that Yeshua was descended through this line.

Despite *halachic* conclusions, the Jewish Bible records the mixed history of the Jewish people, including the promise to Abraham that he would be father to many *goyim,* Gentile nations, and that Israel would be a light to the *goyim.* Yet *halachic* interpretation has often prevailed, rendering as non-Jews fully half to three-quarters of the children and grandchildren of intermarriage.

But Albright's parents were both Jewish, so how do we understand that she was raised as a non-Jew?

Up From the Depths of Despair

It is difficult to plumb the depths of despair and tragedy faced by those who experienced Hitler's death camps, and, even more so, it is beyond our grasp to fully understand the haunting fear survivors must face.

None of us is exempt from the shaping influences of true terror. It is naïve and inhumane to dismiss a parent's desire to protect his children from the hatred that had almost claimed his own Jewish life. We are unfair when we reduce such motivations to shame and embarrassment, as if their Jewishness had been simply an inconvenience. Given the price the Holocaust victims paid and their profound suffering, we cannot sit in judgment, insisting that they should have chosen to die, or at least that they would make that choice for their children.

It was Hitler who degraded and dehumanized the Jews, attempting to strip away every aspect of dignity. None of us must join in the judging of those Jews who survived and concluded that they must take every step necessary to guard their children, even if that meant hiding from their own children the fact of their family's Jewishness.

Viktor Frankl, himself a Holocaust survivor, describes in his book, *Man's Search for Meaning,* the impact such dehumanization had upon himself and other camp survivors:

> "Freedom"—we repeated to ourselves, and yet we could not grasp it. We had said this word so often during all the years we dreamed about it, that it had lost its meaning. . . . We came to meadows full of

flowers. We saw and realized that they were there, but we had no feelings about them. . . . In the evening when we all met again in our hut, one said secretly to the other, "Tell me, were you pleased today?"

And the other replied, feeling ashamed as he did not know that we all felt similarly, "Truthfully, no!" We had literally lost the ability to feel pleased and had to relearn it slowly. . . . Psychologically, what was happening to the liberated prisoners could be called "depersonalization." Everything appeared unreal, unlikely, as in a dream.[1]

Despite this tragic history and the protectiveness it engendered even at the expense of Jewish self-identification, God is calling the Jewish people back to Himself, even the hidden Jews. We see this prominently in the former Soviet Union, but it is becoming increasingly frequent in Eastern Europe, South America, and even in the United States.

Lyda is a red-headed woman, twenty years old, clever and talented. Raised as a Ukrainian, she was given her mother's Russian name at birth. It was another act of protection, a parent wanting to spare her child from an anti-Semitic world. A leader in a Christian church in Zhitomir, some two hours from Kiev, Lyda came in contact with the Messianic Jewish movement in 1997. It was a "cold shower" to her, shocking and unchosen. This was nothing she had anticipated or prepared for. Still, like all cold showers, this one awakened her, and now she is helping build a Messianic Jewish community in her city.

The Jews of Russia and Ukraine and the other Soviet countries faced three kinds of anti-Semitism. The first was the Soviet government's official hostility to Jews who sought to embrace their identity by learning and practicing Judaism or by seeking to emigrate to Israel. This was the political anti-Semitism of the communist era that resulted in lost jobs, demotion, the Gulag, forced relocation, arrest, imprisonment, psychiatric confinement of political opponents, the stripping away of a citizen's rights, and fearing the State as adversary of the Jews.

The second was the common people's hostility to Jews, who were regarded with suspicion and hatred—first, because they came from a different ethnic group, and second, because they were traditionally blamed for the crucifixion of Jesus. Though a Jew may have lived for generations in Russia or Ukraine, spoken the language of his country, been educated in her schools, dressing and eating according to her customs, he was never identified as a Russian or a Ukrainian, always as a Jew. Jewishness was not simply a religious identity; it was a national identity. The Jews were a people, and so they were not the same as the Russian or Ukrainian peoples. In this form of anti-Semitism, the culture and religion of the people conjoined, with Catholic and Orthodox priests agreeing on the un-chosenness of the Jewish people. Jews stood separately as a people apart in both the tsarist and communist eras.

The third force of anti-Semitism belonged to Hitler, who had nearly succeeded in his plan to cleanse the world of the Jews. "We came in by the front gates," one concentration camp survivor wrote, "and we left through the chimneys." Though Hitler was gone, the spirit that animated him lived on, as did so many of his accomplices. And what can we say of all those who stood by silently and passively during the "time of Jacob's trouble?" *When and to where would Hitler's ghost return?* survivors wondered.

How could anyone be certain that another Hitler would not rise up? How could anyone be sure that anti-Semitism would not again take on its violent nature? How reasonable, then, for Jews to hide away their identities, especially for their children's sake.

DEALING WITH THE GUILT OF SURVIVING

Survivors must deal with the guilt they feel for their own lives. "Why should I have lived," a survivor asks, "when my dear, innocent mother or wonderful grandfather perished?" If only to spare their own children the truth of their own nightmarish past, it could be justified. "Even more," a survivor reasons, "I must spare my child the future, however slight the possibility, of another Holocaust."

The former Soviet Union and Eastern Europe are filled with hidden Jews. In these times of relative safety, parents are beginning to tell their children the truth of their ancestry. In my congregation in Rochester were two hidden children, both raised in Germany during World War II by Gentiles willing to keep their secret. This set them on a certain life course that ultimately led them to a Messianic congregation where they could live as Jews who trust in Yeshua.

In South America and throughout the Spanish-speaking world are the descendants of the *marranos* and *conversos.* Faced with banishment from Spain and Portugal during the Inquisitions, their ancestors publicly converted to Christianity. Yet they secretly kept their Jewishness alive at home. However, in the Gentile milieu, their Jewishness inevitably diluted through the generations. Today there are immense numbers of Hispanics whose family rituals included the lighting of candles on Friday evening and other Jewish practices. As they delve into the implications of a Jewish ancestry, they often find themselves among suspicious Jews who wonder whether these are "Jewish wannabes," a derisive term that describes people who will do anything to prove they are Jewish. Yet we must not become cynical or closed to the historic tragedy of our people. Nor can we ignore the unrelenting initiative of God to restore the lost identity of his people.

Israel finally came to terms with the Jewish Ethiopians, and in a massive airlift in 1990 brought thousands of Ethiopians to Israel. The airlift was called "Operation Solomon" in honor of ancient Israel's king who had befriended the Queen of Sheba and, according to Ethiopian history, sired the ancestors of today's Ethiopian Jews. The apostle Philip's encounter with the Ethiopian eunuch gives credence to the idea that there were Ethiopians in ancient times who were going up to Israel to worship and learn.

Jim and Ana Copening have served among the Ethiopian Jews living in Israel. They introduced us to wonderful young Ethiopian Israelis, who have what might only be described as three unusual characteristics. They are Jewish, they are black, and they believe in Yeshua. With sincerity and dedication, they face the mountainous challenge of fitting into the mainstream of Israeli Jewish life. David Korngreen, the retired high-school principal of the posh Israeli suburb *Ra'anana,* told us this task of fitting in will only take a few hundred years.

Nearly every week, I meet someone who has just discovered their Jewish ancestry. It is not always a pleasant experience for them. Consider two cases of Christian leaders, both of whom discovered that their fathers were Jewish. However, they learned this late in life, and they found a tragic element as well. They discovered that the one whom they knew as their grandfather was really a step-grandparent. In each case, their grandmothers had become pregnant out of wedlock by a Jewish man. Unwilling or unable to marry, they took pains to keep the truth secret. And they succeeded. However, God in His own wisdom and timing wanted these two leaders to know of their own Jewishness. So the family secrets were revealed and now each is grappling with the implications of Jewishness on their lives. *What claim,* they must wonder, *does my Jewishness make? How must I respond?* Only in time will they find their answers.

So with these we have a second kind of hidden Jew, the one hidden away, not because of anti-Semitism, but because of illegitimacy and family shame.

DEALING WITH THE FEAR OF ANTI-SEMITISM

Then there is a third kind of hidden Jew. These are the Jews who know their Jewishness. However, because they have fitted into Gentile Christian churches, they hide their identities for fear of anti-Semitism. I first encountered this when teaching in the former Soviet Union. A woman told me that she and other Jewish believers kept their identities secret in their church because of fear of anti-Semitism from fellow church members. This woman was part of a Charismatic church and, to my surprise, I discovered her husband was the senior pastor.

Because so many Christians believe that they have replaced Israel, and because so many pastors and teachers think of Pharisees and other Jewish leaders as being nothing more than religious hypocrites and legalists, many Jews in churches slowly come to understand that their Jewishness is not perceived as a good thing. Fearful of any confrontation, they simply go into hiding rather than separate from their church families.

Eventually, they may take on a sort of self-hating anti-Semitism themselves. During one seminar I gave on Messianic Judaism, a young Jewish leader told me that he recently had to deal with anti-Semitic attitudes in his own heart. Somehow he had picked up this attitude in his Christian church, the result of unrecognized negative attitudes toward the Jews, combined with a tendency to use Jewish biblical examples only in the negative in teaching. Hypocrites, legalists, and opponents to the faith are all identified as Jews, while apostles, pastors, disciples, and heroes of the faith are seldom identified as Jews.

I believe that Christian leaders can learn from both Messianic leaders and from other Christians about how to appreciate the Jewish roots of their faith and how to visibly demonstrate this appreciation. They can also learn to pass this love on to their church members. Ulf Ekman and Carl-Gustaf Severin, along with their network of Word of Life churches in Sweden and the former Soviet Union, have led the way. These churches are vibrantly committed to loving the Jewish people, and it has filtered down to the grassroots level. While many pastors are personally Christian Zionists, few have successfully communicated that to the hearts and minds of their congregation. Word of Life stands as an exception, worthy of imitation in this regard.

My friend, Oleg Scherbakov, a pastor in Nikolaev, Ukraine, is another exception. Oleg has a depth of understanding and commitment to Messianic Jews that is exceptional. God has used him to raise up many leaders for the Messianic Jewish movement and is using him to help plant Messianic congregations with us. During times of great need, Oleg and his leaders helped the Messianic congregation in nearby Odessa, bringing worship teams, dancers, teachers, and even ushers to help establish the fledgling congregation.

Oleg is at the forefront of a new breed of pastors who will be used apostolically to raise up, strengthen, and put in order autonomous Messianic Jewish congregations. If in history God used Jews to help the Gentiles build their churches, how much more can He use Gentiles to help build Messianic synagogues? Oleg is now helping plant a Messianic congregation in his city.

So, Why the Holocaust?

Why did the Holocaust take place? Where was God during the Holocaust? How can there be a God, given the Holocaust? These are the questions that occupy survivors and their descendants, along with all Jews.

Some answers trouble me deeply. I reject the reasoning popularized by Rabbi Harold Kushner in his book, *When Bad Things Happen to Good People,* because he reduces God either to *less than good* or to *less than all-powerful.* Since *less than good* won't work, the God of Israel is left as an impotent demigod. I also reject the reasoning that the Holocaust was simply the inevitable outcome of historic disobedience, a position that depends on blessings and curses. (See Deuteronomy 29–30.) According to this line of thought, all the things that the Jewish people ever suffered were the result of their having come under the curse of God. Those advocating this position recall the terrible suffering of losses experienced by the Jews at other times in history, the exiles and the destruction of Jerusalem being the most noteworthy.

To simplify, the first argument is that the Holocaust was the result of God's inability to be strong and good. The second argument is that God is so good and holy, yet wrathful, that He turned the Jewish people over to punishment and destruction.

While these positions deserve an honest, reasoned response, I find myself unable to reply in such manner. Instead, something passionate, even angry, rises up in me. On occasion I have tried to control it, or at least to make it look polite. But I think I cannot do even this. Perhaps I know why.

First, both these approaches shift the blame, one onto God, the other onto the Jewish people. In other words, the wicked, evil perpetrators are exonerated, and a good God and His people are excoriated. This ignites my own anger. It is like blaming women and children for the violence they suffer at the hands of angry, uncontrolled, vicious husbands and fathers. I will have nothing of it.

Second, it doesn't square with the facts. Jews of every kind were taken to the death camps. It is not true that all unbelievers died and only the faithful were saved. That would have been the case if this were simply divine justice being meted out. However, terribly sinful Jews (and non-Jews, if it needs to be said) were spared, and merciful, kind, God-fearing Jews were reduced to smoke and ashes. It is not true that the better people suffered less atrocities, and the worse suffered more. This is not the hand of impartial justice meting out proportionate punishment. Every kind of Jew was killed at the hands of the Nazis: innocent children, nursing mothers, devout Jewish Catholics, Jewish priests, Jewish nuns, rabbis, Messianic Jews, Hebrew Christians, the saints of the community, along with her sinners.

I think the explanation is far simpler.

In the vision I had on December 21, 1991, I saw the Lord with uplifted hands, pronouncing favor to Zion. From His heavenly realm to the earth below, His words resounded and filled up everything. History was caused by the words that proceeded from His mouth. With His heavenly proclamation, the Zionist appeal to return to the land was sent, heard, and acted upon. Waves of Jews made *aliyah* from the lands of exile to the Land of the Promise. Even the United Nations heard somehow, agreeing with Him by vote and partition to give back to the Jews their ancient homeland. His words continued to shake the earth, bringing with it the reunification of Jerusalem and this lovely city's return to the Jewish people. And the Word continues to define our destinies, with thousands upon thousands of Jewish people gladly receiving the Good News of Yeshua.

It is with this in mind that I assert what is the simplest and, I believe, most true explanation of the Holocaust. When God in His heavenly realm, according to His unsearchable wisdom and sense of right timing, began to declare "Favor to Zion," it loosed more than a century of blessings upon the Jewish people. However, it was also met with an unparalleled response from the adversary of God and the Jewish people. I assert that the Holocaust is simply the outworking on earth of a spiritual battle taking place both in our realm and in the heavenly realm. With God pronouncing favor, and the enemy loosing commensurate destruction, we are witnesses, as is history.

Christians in England and Europe were prophetically stirred to announce in the mid-1800s that the Jewish people would be regathered to their land, accompanied by an outpouring of the Spirit. Following this, there was the birth of Zionism, with Herzl's fateful conference in 1897. During this same time, *pogroms,* violent attacks against Jewish people, increased in number and severity in the region of today's former Soviet Union. Again, we witness favor and destruction battling for supremacy.

Following World War I, *aliyah* continued, and the Ottoman Turkish hegemony over the Middle East was broken. Britain assumed dominion, and with her army came many strong Christians with a respect and love for the Jewish people. British Captain Orde Wingate would train Jewish soldiers during the cover of night, cheering and compelling them on with his chant, "Run, you Lions of Judah!" Wingate taught the Jews how to fight, how to arm themselves, and how to organize themselves. His motivation was simple. God wanted the Jewish people in their promised land, and they must not be victims of resistance or their own inexperience. Favor on one hand, opposition on the other.

Throughout Europe, thousands of Jews were being revived by the Spirit, the first wave of gospel impacting the Jewish people in those lands. From Kishnev to Odessa, from Minsk to Kiev, the Jews were responding to the Good News . . . *Favor.* . . . Yet opposition rose up viciously, first among the Nazis, then among their collaborators in the same lands in which the Jewish people were finding haven and life.

God had always promised to preserve a remnant of the Jewish people. He warned nations not to turn against the Jews, and He promised to defend them when attacked. And He took on yet again that pattern of sacrificial suffering spoken of in Isaiah 53. As Yeshua died for the transgressions of His people, so His people died for the transgressions of the people in whose countries they lived. Not an atoning death, like Yeshua's, but one that nevertheless confronted the world with the extent of human hatred and depravity and the enormity of anti-Semitism in the world.

Though Hitler promised to destroy the Jews, he himself was destroyed—and the Jews live on. And out of the dust of death that fell from the smokestacks of the concentration camps have come the State of Israel and the ever-growing spiritual revival of the Jewish people.

The battle, of course, is not over. When will the

Palestinians fulfill their promise to rescind the PLO charter that commits to the destruction of Israel? When will the skinheads, the neo-Nazis, and the Pamyat Russians abandon their anti-Semitism? When will the anti-Semitic slurs, jokes, and theologies be purged from Christendom and her churches? When will the self-hating of the Jews cease, to be replaced by God-loving?

None of us knows the day or the hour of Yeshua's coming. But in a sense, He has spent the century preparing to come, and the forces of hell have rallied against Him. Yet He *will* come, and Israel will be redeemed, and the nations will be discipled, and His kingdom will be established. *May His kingdom come speedily and in our day.*

אלוהים מביט מטה

GOD LOOKING DOWN

....

Adam was created [last of all beings] on the eve of the Sabbath.
Why? . . . So that if a person becomes too proud, one can say to
him, "The gnat was created before you."
—BABYLONIAN TALMUD, SANHEDRIN 38A

CHAPTER
EIGHT

THE PLANE WAS FLYING SMOOTHLY SEVERAL MILES ABOVE THE former Soviet Union as I read from the prophet Ezekiel:

You have not strengthened the weak or healed the sick or bound up the injured. You have not brought back the strays or searched for the lost. You have ruled them harshly and brutally. So they were scattered because there was no shepherd, and when they were scattered they became food for all the wild animals. My sheep wandered over all the mountains and on every high hill. They were scattered over the whole earth, and no one searched or looked for them. Therefore, you shepherds, hear the word of the LORD: As surely as I live, declares the Sovereign LORD, because my flock lacks a shepherd and so has been plundered and has become food for all the wild animals, and because my shepherds did not search for my flock but cared for themselves rather than for my flock, therefore, O shepherds, hear the word of the LORD: This is what the Sovereign LORD says: I am against the shepherds and will hold them accountable for my flock. I will remove them from tending the flock so that the shepherds can no longer feed themselves. I will rescue my flock from their mouths, and it will no longer be food for them. For this is what the Sovereign LORD says: I myself will search for my sheep and look after them. As a shepherd looks after his scattered flock when he is with them, so will I look after my sheep. I will rescue them from all the places where they were scattered on a day of clouds and darkness. I will bring them out from the nations and gather them from the countries, and I will bring them into their own land. I will pasture them on the mountains of Israel, in the ravines and in all the settlements in the land. I will tend them in a good pasture, and the mountain heights of Israel will be their grazing land. There they will lie down in good grazing land, and there they will feed in a rich pasture on the mountains of Israel. I myself will tend my sheep and have them lie down, declares the Sovereign LORD. I will search for the lost and bring back the strays. I will bind up the injured and strengthen the weak, but the sleek and the strong I will destroy. I will shepherd the flock with justice.

—EZEKIEL 34:4–16, NIV

Though there was no turbulence in the air, something was agitated within me. For a moment, I had a glimpse of God's perspective: I saw so many of the Jewish men and women I knew as if they were sheep without a shepherd. Though so many of them are capable, professionals, leaders in their communities, I understood spiritually that they had been abandoned in a sense.

Many of them were active in their synagogues, holding office, serving the needs of the Jewish community. But inside their souls were holes of emptiness and unfulfilled spiritual hunger. Their rabbis and teachers had led them for years through the rote of liturgical worship but failed to bring them into intimate communion with their God.

I say this as a member of the family, not as some outsider. And I say it with a sense of objectivity that is confirmed in a peculiar way. The Jewish press, writing about Messianic Judaism, has in recent years taken notice of the fulfilled spiritual sense that many Messianic Jews demonstrate. Articles in Jewish magazines have featured challenges to the Jewish community to recognize this spiritual hole within its many members and to find ways of addressing it. Of course, their warning is that if the traditional Jewish community doesn't address Jewish spirituality, then the Messianic Jewish community will win many more Jews into its fold. This is certainly true.

Though many Jews are satisfied in their own Jewishness, very few are satisfied in their spirituality. That's why so many Jews look to the exotic religions of the Far East for spiritual guidance or to the melange of spirituality within the New Age movement. It is why Jews are overrepresented within the many cults of America.

There is a profound Jewish hunger for God, and unless it is directed toward Him, it will be satisfied with some sort of counterfeit spirituality or any of the many false idols that can captivate our loyalty. This hunger for God is often so tragically ignored in the traditional religious institutions of the Jewish community that Judaism has in too many ways been reduced from the radical claims of its origins. God laid claim to Abraham, Isaac, and Jacob. He covenanted with Moses and all of Israel in the Sinai. He promised a king and a kingdom to the line of David. He called the Jewish people to renew their covenant with Him, to know Him personally and intimately, and to allow Him to write His *Torah* on their hearts and minds. He promised to forgive Israel's sins. What does the Lord desire of you? The prophet answers: "To do justly, and to love mercy, and to walk humbly with thy God" (Mic. 6:8). God has a claim on the life of every Jew. It is a claim to a relationship, however far away from God that Jew might be. No matter how far he may have distanced himself from God or his people, yet God calls to him.

"I will regather you," the Lord promises.

LIKE SHEEP

But for now, the Jewish people are still scattered, still like sheep without a shepherd. When the gravity of that condition became clear to me, I was flying out of Russia, headed home to the United States. What a tragic and regretful situation. Deep within the Jewish psyche is a need that can only be met by God Himself. My heart pounded with passion for my own people. O, God's great love, His longing to be gracious, His patience and mercy are all waiting to be expressed without measure to His people.

And for now, so many Jews languish in sorrow or near depression. God looks upon them and suffers with them. Their sorrow is indeed His own sorrow. Their affliction has become His affliction. God's heart yearns for the return of His son. Until then, He grieves, yet He hopes for that eventful day when He—like the prodigal's father standing on the porch—looks into the distance yet once more, this time seeing, yes, this time seeing His lost son making his way up the winding path to his home. It will be a celebration. Life from the dead. "My son who was lost is now found. My son who was dead now lives." But for now the Lord's heart aches with longing.

Uganda? You're Kidding!

Who could build
the Temple
in Uganda?
Uganda,
they're kidding us.
Is Jerusalem in
Uganda?

Or did God call Abram
to Uganda?
Did Moses say,

Let's go down to
Uganda?
Who are you kidding anyway?

Is it Abraham, Isaac, and Uganda?
Did Jacob change his name to
Uganda?
Does Uganda mean
"God-wrestler?"

Maybe you could
move the king there
instead:
Your king,
not mine.
Mine lives in Jerusalem.
Even the British
can't change that.

—SANDY LEVINE

Uganda? You're Kidding! That's the title of a poem my wife wrote, mocking the so-called "Uganda Plan" of the British. Conceived in 1903, it was a British attempt to provide a happy solution for the problem of a Jewish homeland—happy, that is, for the Arabs. It would give the Jews a homeland in Africa, and Palestine would be given to the Arabs. For a time Theodor Herzl even favored the plan as the best the Jews could hope for, given the political realities and the desperate need the Jewish people had for a place of their own.

But hoping against hope and resisting the Crown and their Arab neighbors, the Jews persevered, willing to accept nothing less than some of the land promised to Abraham, Isaac, and Jacob.

"My king lives in Jerusalem. Even the British can't change that. Was it Abraham, Isaac, and Uganda?" Sandy wrote.

This dogged determination to receive the promise of the

land was characteristic of the *chalutzim,* the "pioneers" of Israel who came from Western, Central, and Eastern Europe up to and including Russia, Ukraine, and the Pale of Settlement, that territory under Russian rule where Jews were confined from the late 1700s to the early 1900s. These Zionist pioneers embraced the land with hope and passion. They drained mosquito-infested, malaria-incubating swamps and turned the arid desert into "well-watered gardens." *Dor l'dor,* from generation to generation, the hope of the return had been passed.

Galut

What we call in English the *Diaspora,* or "dispersion," is known in Hebrew as the *Galut,* the "exile." When Jews were driven out of their homeland and forced to dwell in the lands of their conquerors, they were exiled, banished from the land of their fathers. But as the wise woman from Tekoa said, "God does not take away life; instead, he devises ways so that a banished person may not remain estranged from him" (2 Sam. 14:14, NIV). Whether His hand moves slowly or quickly, God is always working to bring His people back to Himself and to the promised land.

Abraham lived in Egypt for a time, but Isaac couldn't. Jacob moved there, looking for food during a famine, finding that and even more—his son Joseph, once dead but now found. Yeshua spent His infancy there, or perhaps better, His toddler years. But for the Jews, Egypt is no destination. It may be a hiding place, but it gives no permanent freedom. It is *Mitzraim,* the "straits," a narrow, difficult place, even if less difficult than famine or death. It is a temporary place, a place to leave. And in a sense, Europe was like Egypt for the Jews.

Though 90 percent of the world's Jews lived in Europe, it was no place of real safety. The threat of *pogroms* and the reality of discrimination persevered. As in Babylon, the Jews in Europe found solace and solidarity in study, making

their schools, the *yeshivot,* the center of community and tradition, and seeking through them to preserve and extend
the wisdom of the sages. On one side, they gave themselves to separation—from the Gentiles—and to study, and
on the other side, Jews sought to be accepted and to assim-
ilate. Czar Alexandre III thought that the Jewish problem
would be solved in thirds. One-third would be killed, one-
third would leave Russia, one-third would convert to
Christianity—forsaking their Jewish identities.

In Europe, the Jews were still in exile. As the former chief
rabbi of England recently noted, in Western Europe—the
land of the Enlightenment—Judaism became *a religion
without a people,* while in Eastern Europe, the Jews became
a people without a religion.

In 167 B.C., the Syrian-Greeks invaded Israel, and the
Seleucid emperor, Antiochus Epiphanes, yet another impe-
rial man-god, took the Jerusalem temple captive. Profaned
with pig blood and sacrifice, the temple was dedicated to
Zeus, and the emperor's eagle's insignia was mounted at
the temple entrance. The sovereignty of the God of Israel
was challenged, and the pagans were, for a time, victorious.

Under Antiochus, the Jews were allowed to remain in the
land, but they were expected to abandon their religious distinctives and express uncompromised loyalty both to the
state and the religion of the state.

Jewish identity was assaulted, seen correctly as a threat to
the state's interest and hegemony. Jews were forbidden to
possess the five Books of Moses, the *Torah.* Circumcision of
the sons on the eighth day was banned in an attempt to cut
off the Jews from their peculiar identity as a people with a
covenant sign that had been given to their father Abraham.
And the Jews were forced to eat pork, against their biblical
dietary law.

Many assimilated—some by preference, some by fear—
while others were animated by the cold calculus, counting
the costs and finding them too high. A surgical technique
was devised to reverse the visible effects of circumcision as

the sons of Judah tried to be like the sons of Jovan in the gymnasium, with its naked exercises and athletics. Others took on the minds of their conquerors and barely noticed that their once-biblically based thoughts had been taken captive by the Greek and Roman philosophers and the wisdom of the world.

Those Jews who defied Antiochus were scorned and scourged. They were beaten and tortured. Some were cooked alive in unspeakably horrific and public displays of this barbaric "civilization." Others were hanged or beheaded, mounted on city walls like trophies from the hunt. The tongues of others were cut out, yet they maintained a resolve to live as the Jewish people, or to die freely.

A priestly family, *HaShmonim,* the Hasmoneans, rose up and led a rebellion. Using guerrilla tactics, they eventually defeated and vanquished their oppressors. The temple was cleansed and dedicated to the God of Israel once again. A feast of *Chanukah,* of "Dedication," was celebrated and continues to this day. This holiday does not appear in the *Tanakh,* the Jewish Scriptures, but only in the Books of the Maccabees and, interestingly, in the writings of the apostles. Yeshua Himself, we're told, went to Jerusalem and the temple for the *Chanukah* (John 10:22) celebration, translated into English as the "Feast of Dedication."

So the Jews regained their sovereignty in 142 B.C., but the Hasmoneans proved to be cruel rulers themselves. Intolerant of diversity, under their rule Jews were once again pitted against Jews. When the land became almost ungovernable, the Jewish leaders sought help from Rome and invited her troops and government to still the foment and to prevent a civil war. So in a sense, the Jews turned to Egypt again, looking for the nations with their horses and chariots, their military and political might, to settle the disputes of Jerusalem.

The Romans brought peace, but it was *Pax Romana,* not the *shalom* of the Lord. For a time, as always, the plan worked, but Roman law was not Jewish law, nor was Roman justice Jewish justice. And so, the land of the Jews was governed ultimately by yet another nation. This time the Jews were not exiled from their land, but nevertheless they had sacrificed their autonomy. As always in this drama of many acts, true and counterfeit rose up together in counterpoint. Yeshua the true Messiah came but was deemed false, just as Isaiah the Prophet had foretold. And later came *Bar Kokhba*, the false Messiah, who was proclaimed to be true by the revered Rabbi Akiba. With the death of Yeshua, the curtain was ripped that enclosed the holy of holies in the temple. It was as if God Himself tore His garment in grief. (And with *Bar Kokhbah's* defeat, all of Israel herself was torn.) The Roman general Titus ordered Jerusalem's destruction in A.D./C.E. 70, and Jews were banished from the city, which was renamed *Aelia Capetolina,* yet another attempt to defile and profane Jerusalem, to erase her Jewish identity, and yet another case of the Gentile nations trampling upon the city of the great King.

Israel became Palestine in homage to the Philistines, and the land was consigned to the Romans, the Muslims, the Crusaders, the Turks, and then the British. It was conjoined to the Levant, Lebanon, and was little more than a district of Syria when ruled by the Ottomans. To this day, Syria considers Lebanon hers, as well as most of Israel.

My Israel

In 1965 I visited Israel with my family. As a ten-year-old, I was astonished that we Jews had our own land. We lived in Roanoke, Virginia, one of a few hundred Jewish families, by numbers an insignificant minority. But in Israel we actually had a land—our Jewish homeland. Modern cities were being built on ancient sites, and cities with biblical names rose again from the sands. Construction would halt on many projects because so many attempts to dig for a foundation became potential archaeological excavations: so much history buried beneath the sand, and so much history rising above it.

I remember Jerusalem, divided between Israel and Jordan, with fences separating both sides from a buffer of no-man's land. "Keep your hands off the fence," we were told, "or a soldier will train his gun on you and maybe shoot."

While Rome's Titus had once ordered Jerusalem's destruction, nineteen centuries later England's General George Allenbee entered the city with humility, dismounting his splendid horse to walk on her ancient streets. Yet the government of England was less humble than her General Allenbee, liberating Jerusalem from Turkish rule only to find that Britain could not resist the temptation herself to rule over this city and land that was not hers. Despite an initial promise to give back the land to the Jews and despite the muddled, then rejected compromise of the "Uganda Plan," the British stumbled over Jerusalem, and the land became to her a cup of reeling. The British found the land ungovernable but didn't have the heart or will to crush the Jews militarily. And so she threw down the cup and abandoned the land, and Jewish-Arab warfare inevitably escalated.

"Let the sons of Isaac and the sons of Ishmael fight," the British decided. Miraculously, the sons of Isaac won, and in 1948 the Jewish homeland was recognized as a legitimate nation, though not by the Arab states and their allies.

In 1967 Jerusalem was reunited again by war, and for the first time since Titus, Jews had the right to dwell throughout the city they governed. But in a sense that right was no guarantee.

Jerusalem today is still divided into East and West. Her old city is quartered with Arabs, Christians, Armenians, and Jews, each holding onto their portion. The Palestinian Authority publicly lays claim to the eastern half, if not privately to the whole of Jerusalem. And recent Israeli attempts to build in eastern Jerusalem have been met with Arab outrage and uprising. Again the Jewish people find the danger of exercising sovereignty over their homeland.

And what is the prospect for peace? Who knows for sure? Again the Jews are torn, as is Jerusalem. The Palestinian

Authority has complied with a *fatwah,* an Islamic religious decree, that it is a capital offense for a Muslim to sell Israeli land to a Jew.

I have walked the streets of Jewish Jerusalem with confidence in the past, but I feel unsure and unsafe when I even drive near or through her eastern Arabic side. How will I feel walking again on Ben Yehudah Street, past the site where fifteen died and one hundred sixty were injured in the Hamas-sponsored triple-suicide bombing, which took place just recently? How will I feel in the Jewish market, *Makhaneh Yehudah,* where an earlier terrorist bombing killed and injured so many others? Will I shy away from those places as if they are hexed or cursed? Or will I defy those who want to return us to a captivity where even Jerusalem is trampled on?

I have visited those places where terrorist bombs have exploded before, haunted by loss but not fear. I refuse to hate the Arabs or even to demonize the Muslims. I have no answers, only a yearning. But I have no way of materializing that yearning, and it renders me, as Rabbi Joseph Soleveitchik says, "a lonely man of faith."

TRAMPLING ON JERUSALEM

When will the nations tire of trampling on Jerusalem? If only they already had. But no; they still insist, as if Jerusalem is a prize to be taken or a contest to be won. And so the battle continues. And Israel to this day looks to the nations to give her some type of peace. It reminds me, though, of Jeremiah's lamentation: "Moreover, our eyes failed, looking in vain for help; from our towers we watched for a nation that could not save us" (Lam. 4:17, NIV).

Still I am urged on by the psalmist who entreats me to pray for the *shalom* of Jerusalem, declaring, even pleading for the prosperity of those who love her.

Scattered throughout this wonderful city are Christians and Messianic Jews who count Jerusalem as their home—a precious treasure. Their story, the story of Christians and Messianic Jews, is intertwined and fascinating. How did they come here? What do they do here? What are they looking for?

I was flying home from Russia when I was overtaken with the weight of the condition of the Jewish people. So many sheep without a shepherd, wandering, scattered, subject to vicious attack. My heart broke with the realization that despite every Jewish success, there remains something empty in the Jewish soul. And that void is also in the very heart of God, who longs for the return of His son. God Himself grieves for His lost son. My heart ached with His. Perhaps this is some of the fellowship of His suffering described in Philippians 3:8–11.

"What Do You Want?"

For years I had given myself to the pastoral ministry. In 1992 I joined the Messianic movement and dedicated myself full time to my own people. In 1994, I touched a chord in God's heart that dramatically realigned my efforts. I was in Toronto, at a meeting with hundreds of other believers, many of them pastors. Waiting for someone to pray for me, I leaned up against a pillar and closed my eyes.

"What do you want?" I heard the Lord ask me. It only took a few seconds for my answer to form.

"I want to raise up the shepherds of Israel," I said.

"Okay," the Lord said, "but everywhere you go you must call for them."

That's when I knew what was in God's heart. He was longing for the Jewish people to be pastored. "No longer sheep without a shepherd"—that was His promise. "I will place shepherds over them who will tend them" (Jer. 23:4, NIV), the prophet Jeremiah proclaimed in the name of the Lord. These shepherds will have God's heart, pastoring with love, understanding, and knowledge.

But who would dedicate themselves to identifying,

encouraging, and raising up these shepherds for the Jewish people? Certainly many others would do so, but for me on that August day in 1994, I knew I would have to entirely reorient my life and time toward this end.

Since then, almost wherever I go—any kind of church, every city, every conference, every seminar, every Messianic congregation—I will call for those whose hearts beat with mercy and compassion for the Jewish people. Together Sandy and I will pray for these precious men and women, expecting God to touch their hearts even more deeply. We have been amazed to watch God pour out new measures of anointing upon those who respond.

Sandy and I now dedicate our lives to identifying and raising up the shepherds of Israel. In our work with Hear O Israel Ministries, we focus our attention on the leaders of the Messianic congregations we are planting. God is working to show us who has been called to lead new congregations. We oversee their ministries, helping them succeed in their callings as shepherds for Israel.

SHEPHERDS FOR ISRAEL

These shepherds of Israel are not glory hounds or people with selfish ambitions. Next to the pain of childbirth, there are few things that are harder than ministering to the Jewish people! With centuries of spiritual opposition and a near victory by the enemy yet in this century, everything that is done in Jewish ministry is shrouded in spiritual warfare. These are men and women who are willing to lose some of their own lives in order to see the ultimate regaining of life—life from the dead—by the Jewish people. A people of the Resurrection! Like search teams looking for someone lost in the winter woods, these are people who would sacrifice their own creature comforts and opportunities for enrichment in order to give themselves to helping find just one who is hopelessly lost. For they hope against hope, and their reward comes . . . from the hand of God.

We have seen hundreds of people, Jews and Gentiles together, who have been responding to this peculiar call on their lives. Some of them have gone into full-time ministry. Others are serving as home-group leaders or discipling new believers. Some are working in food kitchens. Others are helping distribute humanitarian aid to needy Jews. Some are helping the Jews get home to Israel. Others are taking care of the Jews who remain in the *Diaspora*.

We are no longer surprised to see tears flowing down the cheeks of those we pray for. Their hearts are being touched by God's heart. Some of these people have been so misunderstood over the years. They may never have fitted into their church setting. When everyone else was focused on one thing, their attention was constantly turned toward the Jewish people. We have been accused of being fanatics, extreme, or excessive. They have been told they had no balance in their lives. Yet the only cause that constantly burned inside with fire was the cause of the Jewish people. I've seen such a marvelous release of joy and healing come upon these people when they come forward to answer the call of the shepherds of Israel. Sandy likes to say, "It's as if they have been issued a permit, and now these people are free to operate in their callings."

A Heart for Israel

In Tartu, Estonia, we had the privilege of ministering in the church pastored by Albert Turnpu. A man of great capacity and vision, Albert's father was Jewish, though Albert was raised without any significant Jewish identity. Through his contact with Ulf Ekman, he grew in his ministry of love to the Jewish people. While ministering at his church on Sandy's birthday in 1997, she and I called for the shepherds of Israel to come forward for ministry.

Sometimes we will pray over an entire group and other times we will pray over individuals. And sometimes we'll pray over both. This time Sandy and I were directed to lay hands on only certain individuals who had come up. In some spiritual way, she and I both recognized each one of these as having been especially called and touched by God. Later that afternoon we were told that every person we laid hands on was already part of a Jewish outreach ministry based in the church. Only those who had already been giving themselves to ministry had manifested the kind of anointing that drew our attention. It was an important lesson. It built their faith and ours that the Holy Spirit would single out these individuals and show them to us. It also reminded us that when we are faithful in what we have been given, we will receive more. I'm grateful that the Lord wants to increase the anointing in all of our lives. I would hate to end my life with the current level of anointing for ministry. I want so much more! Only as I walk in faithfulness, real-time faithfulness, will I grow in that anointing.

And, bless God, when we walk in faithfulness, hearing and obeying His voice, there is a supernatural dimension that operates in our lives. Strongholds in my life are broken. Broken places are healed. Doubts and insecurities are removed. Vision is released. And at the same time this supernaturalness is released in a way that benefits those to whom we minister. What a blessing we have enjoyed to go back a few months or a year or two later and find out that God really did break through in people's lives.

LORD OF THE BREAKTHROUGH

One area where we have had much faith is for those who are childless. We have seen God break through for so many people whose quivers are now full or getting there. At the Passover *seder* in our home in 1991, we had a time for foot-washing and prophetic ministry and prayer. Following Yeshua's pattern of washing the feet before the Passover meal, we have again and again experienced the joy He promised. I will never forget when a prophetic anointing descended as we were washing the feet of one couple we know. An intermarried couple, they had tried for years to have children but had suffered miscarriage and disappointment. On this evening, the word of the Lord was simple and direct—and frighteningly specific.

As the women were washing the woman's feet, they first prayed for her to have a child. Then the prayer shifted into a forceful, prophetic quality, describing the kind of labor she would have as she gave birth.

That kind of specific word either is going to be a blessing or it will bring contempt. In fact, the couple conceived within a month, and their daughter was born before the following Passover. She is an intelligent, beautiful young girl, a miraculous provision of God. Who knows but God how He will use this family to help restore His people?

At the 1995 Messianic rabbi's conference, which is held annually in Florida, Sandy and I sought out two friends of ours. They had long been unable to conceive, yet the maternal and paternal instincts within them were intensifying. God released in us a gift of faith for this dear couple, and we prayed, again with a prophetic declaratory sense. Sometimes faith can rise up in us, a measure of faith that overcomes every contrary indication, every circumstance. Call it mountain-moving faith as Yeshua did, because its power is in its quality, not its quantity. All it takes is some of *this* kind of faith to bring about impossible *change!*

"A hope deferred makes the heart sick," Proverbs says, and something in this woman's heart had grown hard for all the waiting. She had all but given up on her hope. But the Lord gave us a word for them that expressed His own hope for their family. God's hope for their hopelessness. Their own faith enlarged and renewed, they waited expectantly for what God had for them. We rejoiced when we heard the news that they were cleared to adopt a baby girl. Their daughter is our godchild, and we take heart that sometimes God brings children in miraculous and unexpected ways.

FAMILYHOOD RESTORED

These two gifts of faith are related. Calling for the shepherds of Israel is central to God's plan to revive and complete His Jewish people. Praying for those who are barren is central to God's plan to restore familyhood. Both gifts bring life where it is missing or incomplete. Hoping against hope was a hallmark of Abraham's faith. Without wavering, we also hope and pray.

In 1996 we stepped down from our leadership within Congregation Shema Yisrael in order to take on the full-time responsibility to watch over the shepherds of Israel. Our work with Hear O Israel Ministries now involves raising up and overseeing leaders for the Messianic movement, better for the Jewish people. We travel the globe with our eyes open for those individuals and congregations with special callings to be used to revive and restore the Jewish people. We're planting new congregations in the former Soviet Union, in the United States, and, as God leads, in other parts of the world. What a privilege it is to be able to serve in this way!

When Yeshua saw Salome, the mother of the sons of Zebedee, He wanted to know her desire. She was ambitious for her sons, asking that they be given the seats on either side of Yeshua. This He couldn't give, He said, " . . . but it shall be given to them for whom it is prepared of my Father." He said in front of all His disciples, "Whosoever will be great among you, let him be your minister" (Matt. 20:23, 26).

Right after this word on servant leadership, Yeshua and His disciples were leaving Jericho. Two blind men were sitting by the roadside, and when they heard that Yeshua was going by, they shouted, disrupting the peace and calm with the plea for the "Son of David" to have mercy on them. Despite His disciples' efforts to protect Him from such noisy, intrusive men, Yeshua called them to Him and asked what they wanted.

Without hesitation, they asked for their sight. This was immediately granted, and the blind men could see (Matt. 20:29–34). On another occasion, Yeshua granted immediate sight to a man who had been blind since birth. Once blind, now able to see, this young man went throughout the countryside sharing with others what Yeshua had done for him. When others challenged his claims about Yeshua, he stood on his own testimony. "I was blind but now I see!" (John 9:25, NIV).

Few things are as compelling as a good testimony, given in season to the right person. The once-blind young man himself became a disciple of Yeshua's, using his newly gained sight to enable him to follow Him.

If the Lord were to come to you today and ask what you want, would your answer come without hesitation? Would you choose your own promotion, or the promotion of God's kingdom? Would you be willing to *spend yourself* on behalf of His people Israel?

בנים אובדים בימינו

MODERN PRODIGALS

••

If I forget you, O Jerusalem,
let my right hand wither,
let my tongue stick to my palate
if I cease to think of you,
if I do not keep [the destroyed city of] Jerusalem in memory
even at my happiest hour.
—PSALM 137:5–6

CHAPTER
NINE

GOD IS LOOKING FOR A PEOPLE LOOKING AT HIM. THAT'S WHY Yeshua could say, "I only do what I see the Father doing." Our greatest temptation is to be so busy with what we understand to be the Father's business, that we don't observe what the Father is actually doing. The parable of the prodigal son is a parable of the kingdom of God. (See Luke 15.) That means that its lessons are not bound by time or space, or applicable to one narrow situation.

In this parable, Yeshua tells us about a father with two sons, one who was faithful, staying at home and working in his father's business. The other son was not so ardent, abandoning the family and taking his share of his inheritance even before his father had died. Only after he had spent all he had, falling into one of life's nasty gutters, did he come to his senses.

Impoverished though he was, the younger son was enriched with a new sense of belonging. He belonged to his father, and his future even as his father's slave would be better than his reckless independence. So he returned home to discover that his father was waiting for him, looking into the distance for just such a time as this when he would return. Humbled and broken, he fell at his father's feet, tears of sorrow anointing his patient parent. But the father was filled with gladness, for the son he had lost was now returned, the one whom he considered as good as dead was now alive again. "Celebrate with a feast of succulent veal," the father called out.

Alongside the elder brother came, not able to enter into the joy. Feeling rejected and devalued, he brought forth a complaint. "Father, you never did this for me, yet I have been faithful."

"Son, all I have is yours. Rejoice with me," the father replied.

This parable of the kingdom was heard by Yeshua's contemporaries in one way. Perhaps they were the elder brother, faithful and true to their Father in heaven. But these prostitutes, drunkards, tax collectors, and Gentiles following after Yeshua—they were the younger brother, a squanderer.

Today, I think the parable can be heard differently. Sandy shared this insight with me in February 1988. She saw a vast well-kept property, a beautiful house on a ranch, not unlike the ranch home on the television series, *Bonanza*. All about, ranch hands were busy taking care of business. Hardest working among them was the elder brother. He was the church, busy about the Father's business, doing everything he was supposed to do, ever mindful of his own faithfulness.

But he didn't notice that his Father would return again and again to stand on that porch. The elder brother didn't ask what or for whom his Father was looking. He was too busy being faithful, doing things right, to notice.

Yet day after day, the Father would stand on that porch, leaning into the railing, staring down the long, winding road. Sandy saw this Father as one with immense dignity and authority. Silver-haired, with such presence and stature, not unlike Ben Cartwright. Despite this important habit of faithfulness, the elder brother failed to plumb the depths of his Father's heart.

And who then is the younger brother today, if not Israel, the Jewish people? Many in the church look down upon the Jewish people, mindful of Israel's unfaithfulness, yet insecure in their own relationship with the Father.

If we only had to choose between being the elder brother

or the younger brother, which would we take? Fortunately, there is a third choice. In this hour, God is looking for those who are looking at Him. "Who," He asks, "will stand on the porch with Him, using their free time to look for the return of that wandering son? Who will keep the Lord company, occupied with Him as He anticipates that this younger son will come home? Who will have the Father's heart?"

Ask yourself this: When the Jewish people began to make their way down the road home to the Father, were you standing and watching with Him? Were you busy doing something else, as if the return of the son meant so little? Did the Father's unwavering hope stir you, or did you find it trivial? Were you engrossed in programs and activities, or did you look at Him and do what you saw Him doing?

God is looking for men and women, secure in their own relationship with Him, who will simply watch and take note of the fact that He is standing on the porch, looking for the return of Israel. It is time to rise up to our calling as sons and relate to the matters of our Father's heart.

Yeshua's parable ends with the elder brother standing alone in the yard. It seems he just couldn't find his way into the party. Where are you standing today? Are you out in the yard, unable to enter in? Or are you by the Father's side, happy with Him that your brother is back?

When I recast the parable of the good Samaritan in modern terms, I think of the man beaten on the side of the road as a Jew. (See Luke 10:30–37.) Those who pass him by are Christians, one a noted pastor hurrying to his four Sunday morning services to speak to his overflowing congregation; another a respected worship leader, determined to get to the prayer meeting before the big conference he's helping to lead. And the one who stops to help this bloodied victim is a Mormon who, like the Samaritan, has changed things just enough that the truth as we know it has been distorted with just too much error and additions. In that retelling, it's the Mormon, but it could be a New Ager who is neighborly and the believers who all have mud on their faces.

Sandy has challenged me to think of this in a fresh new way. What if the one beaten and robbed was Yeshua? What if the story He told is really His own story—not an allegory about His time on this earth, but a piece of simple biography? What if He was walking from Jerusalem down to the Dead Sea, passing through that dangerous hilly area where robbers would hide? Maybe Yeshua was walking that long downhill trek when He was approached by a couple of men who made polite conversation, found out where He was headed and that no one was with Him. Maybe then they struck Yeshua, and He fell to the ground. Maybe they beat Him, not because of His resistance, but simply because of the hatred in their hearts for that which was innocent and good. What if Yeshua was robbed and mugged, viciously kicked and beaten, left lying on the side of the road, moaning, dirty, caked in His own drying blood? What if it really was a priest who walked by without concern? What if another leader avoided taking note of his fellow man, hurrying away in order to avoid contact with that person who probably had done something terrible to be in such a God-awful state. And what if the only person who did stop for Him was a Samaritan, an unclean half-Jew, who had a different Bible and a different doctrine? Imagine this is the story of Yeshua and the Samaritan. What a shocking example of pathos this would be. And who in this story had neighborly love? A Samaritan.

The Father's Heart

These parables together work to undo our simplistic religiosity and to reconnect us with the absolute truth of the Father's heart. Where is our own heart? Is it turned to the Father and His Son, or to something else? No matter how religious it might look, unless our fervor is God-directed it will be judged, just as the elder son's heart was judged and just as the passersby were judged.

These are genuine questions we must ponder for ourselves, because we have no one who has gone before us who can show us the path. What God wants to do between Jews and non-Jews, between Christians and Messianic Jews, has no simple precedent. We cannot simply follow in the footsteps of those who have gone before. Certainly there are some bright lights we could look to, and they can be our inspirations. But, in fact, the situation is too new, and the path has not yet been fully beaten.

So God is looking for those of us who are willing to beat the path down ourselves so that others can follow. Sometimes the days ahead look like the underbrush of a southwest Virginia forest, filled with briars and other sticky bushes. How easy it would be to simply turn around and to walk alongside the road. But for me and for many others, we are responding to a call that requires that we keep the destination always in mind because the road is not yet built. We are beating the path as we go.

Beating the path requires endurance, thick skin, and a bit of stubbornness—at least enough to refuse the counsel of the "wise" who would tell us we're walking in the wrong direction. But we know we're headed in the right direction, and that we're aiming for the right destination: We're going to Jerusalem! And so we steadfastly resolve to keep our eyes focused on Yeshua. Even if this race bogs down a bit on foot, we will keep running to the end where we will claim our prize.

What You Can Do — Right Now

Social psychologists have noted a major difference between those who are high achievers and those who underachieve. The high achievers set many goals—small goals that they accomplish, then move on to the next goal. Thus they assure themselves of constant progress. The underachievers, however, set fewer goals and make them much larger. Now, I'm not talking about the issue of vision so much as I am about the actions we take towards accomplishing that vision. Two people can see the same thing, but one will be a visionary and the other a dreamer. The first will move forward, *accomplishing* something every day that moves him closer toward the goal of the vision. The second will *fantasize* about his future glory, looking at his dream with much admiration and with little action. Yes, his words will be lofty and, for some, inspirational, but in the end nothing will have changed. Because the dreamer is an underachiever.

If we are going to see our own little part of the world changed, it will not be by dreams alone. It will take action too. Those who put actions to their dreams are the true visionaries. So it is with the revival of the Jewish people. I've met so many people who frolic after one "new truth," then another. They're caught up in the minutiae of life, self-absorbed in esoterica. But real change is brought about by those who *do something today* and again tomorrow. Those who continue to take one more step will be the enduring ones. "Those who endure to the end," Yeshua said, "will be saved." That Greek word for "end," *telos,* means more than "the end of the line." It means "the purpose, the ultimate goal." Salvation is for those who endure by concentrating on the purpose and God's ultimate goal.

If we are going to accomplish real change in this world, if we are going to be participants in this great End-Time revival of the Jewish people, we must take action—step by step.

DOING SOMETHING, RATHER THAN NOTHING

Perhaps the only unforgivable thing we could do is *nothing.* Any action on behalf of Jewish restoration is commendable, even if not all are equal. Still, what is most important is that we think wisely and are led by the Spirit, doing something, anything, to help. When the Jewish people were being slaughtered by the millions, every action, every effort of rescue was commendable. If some saved more than others, that is what we understand and expect. The only unforgivable posture was to do nothing. When the people are being led to slaughter, we must intervene somehow. We simply cannot be bystanders again. During the Holocaust, every simple act of kindness was worthy. That's why Yeshua could say that we had fed Him, clothed Him, and visited Him in prison. *When did we do this?* we wonder. He answers, "When you did this to the least of these My brothers. As the Jews were singled out for extermination, they indeed became the least of these My brothers." The least of these—those not able to draw on their own strength for help. My brothers—members of Yeshua's own family—worthy of being rescued.

CONCRETE IDEAS FOR WHAT WE CAN DO

No one could suggest to you that your calling is to carry out Jewish men and women in sacks, taking them past the Nazis into safety and claiming to be carrying dead swine. This is what Pastor Nikolai's grandfather did in Belarus, and only the Holy Spirit could have empowered him for this ministry. No one could simply assign that to a fellow human and expect the other to take it up. It was a divine calling to rescue so many Jews from Nazi execution. So many aspects of life in ministry are like that.

So if it is futile in our natural strength to call other people to such risk, it is not futile to expect those whom God has called to take such risks. For the rest of us, I offer the following thoughts about some good things to do. You'll notice that many of them are slanted toward the kind of activities that I have been involved in. This is, I believe, a result of my own sense of accomplishment and satisfaction and my awareness of how others have been similarly fulfilled.

TRAILBLAZING

After we blaze a path, others will follow. I've spent many

hours walking in various parks, and none compare to those in the Blue Ridge Mountains of Virginia. With awesome vistas, majestic valleys, and lovely peaks, the Blue Ridge Mountains express a friendly welcome to come explore her beauties. When we walk into her woods, adorned with ferns, rhododendrons, mountain laurel, and dogwood, we benefit so much from her trails. The beaten-down places allow us to carefully explore where others have gone. This is the nature of trailblazing. Even if it seems that we are beating the trail alone, others are following. They may begin their journeys after we have ended ours, or some distance may separate us and we may never meet. But everyone who precedes us makes it easier for us to find our way. March on!

And what a joy it is to discover others whose paths intersect with ours. At first we may think theirs was a detour, but often when we join others on their own paths, we find the unexpected. In a sense, as Psalm 107 declares, we are not able to find our way to God's city. But in our distress, we call out to Him, and He leads us straightway. Sometimes the way the Lord leads us is onto someone else's path. In their company, walking in the paths they have beaten before, we enjoy a bit of rest and companionship, the hard work of trailblazing stopping for a moment while we walk in someone else's labor.

I think back to my dream when Sandy and I were walking through abandoned neighborhoods in a city deserted because of war or its threat. Along the way, Sandy found someone who was also headed toward our destination—Jerusalem! She invited him along, and he joined us, though I had first felt the impulse of fear and the desire to protect myself by not getting involved. As I woke up from this dream, I was taken with an important thought: *Sandy will find many who are headed to Jerusalem. She must be free to do this, and I must encourage her because she will be the one, most likely, who will first catch the scent and take the first step in that direction.*

STORIES OF THOSE WHO ARE DOING SOMETHING NOW

Many have gone before us, and it is a privilege to walk in their footsteps. Occasionally we have the privilege of standing on the shoulders of those who are like giants to us, enabling us to see above and beyond. The adventure begins the moment we say to the Lord that we want to carry some of His lovely Jewish sons and daughters home to Him, home to Israel, home to their people. Those of you who do this are kings and queens in His sight, and He will bedeck you with royal garb and dignify you with authority and power. You will be foster fathers and nursing mothers, and your charglings will grow strong and rise up into the fullness of their Jewish calling. As they grow, give them space. They belong to their Father, and as they return to Him, they usher in life from the dead—for themselves, for their families, and for the nations of this world. Finally . . .

> The hand of the LORD was upon me, and carried me out in the spirit of the LORD, and set me down in the midst of the valley which was full of bones, and caused me to pass by them round about: and, behold, there were very many in the open valley; and, lo, they were very dry. And he said unto me, Son of man, can these bones live? And I answered, O Lord God, thou knowest. Again he said unto me, Prophesy upon these bones, and say unto them, O ye dry bones, hear the word of the LORD. Thus saith the Lord God unto these bones; Behold, I will cause breath to enter into you, and ye shall live: And I will lay sinews upon you, and will bring up flesh upon you, and cover you with skin, and put breath in you, and ye shall live; and ye shall know that I am the LORD. So I prophesied as I was commanded: and as I prophesied, there was a noise, and behold a shaking, and the bones came together, bone to his bone.
>
> —EZEKIEL 37:1–7

When I heard the voice of God calling me for the very first time, it completely changed the direction of my life. My encounter with the living God of Israel catapulted me into the supernatural realm of His plan to restore the Jewish people to Himself and to pour out power on us (yet again) so that we could be His witnesses with power to the *eschaton,* the uttermost parts of the earth and the uttermost parts of history—until the very end of the age and the End of Days. It's as if the Lord has sounded a *shofar* blast, and the Jewish dry bones are coming together and being given new life. Ezekiel's vision of the dry bones of Israel is coming to pass.

סוף דבר

EPILOGUE

••

I will restore my people Israel.
They shall rebuild ruined cities and inhabit them;
They shall plant vineyards and drink their wine;
They shall till gardens and eat their fruits.
And I will plant them upon their soil, nevermore to be uprooted
From the soil I have given them, said the Lord your God.
—AMOS 9:14–15

ALL OF US WONDER WHAT WILL HAPPEN TO THE JEWISH PEOPLE IN the former Soviet Union when anti-Semitism rises up in violent hatred. Those of us who are involved with the Jewish people there hope that our sense of timing is accurate. We do not want to be late in detecting when we need to shift our efforts to helping Jews leave. If we are too early, we will be called fanatics or alarmists and we will miss opportunities for evangelism. If we are too late, we will have failed. If we are just a bit early, we will be considered wise. Reputations notwithstanding, we have an obligation to listen carefully to the Holy Spirit, and to one another, as we are finding our way.

In Nazi Germany and Europe right before World War II, there were "dark forebodings and a handful of prophetic utterances," as Matthew Berke notes, but not "a widely recognized public fact capable of shaping policy." Or as another writer observed, it was in part a lack of foresight, "as most Jews could not imagine the terrible fate that awaited them." Whether another Hitler will rise up with an obsession and ability to attempt the genocide of the Jews, there most certainly will rise up again those who are animated with the "Amalek" spirit.

Those who will issue the warning in these coming days must be prepared to be perceived as alarmist and contrarian. It may only be those who perceive "dark forebodings" who will be alert enough to warn us all. It may only be through a "handful of prophetic utterances" that the alarm will be sounded. So let us listen carefully, because all we have to rely upon ultimately is a prophetic sense. It may be again that no government is able to rescue the Jewish people— worse, that no government would even *want to*. It may be that politics may again show its dark side, or just as likely, that the glorious promise of the politicians to save any of us will be shown an illusion, another example of puffed-up pride. As God pulls down every illusion, every falsehood that rears up against the knowledge of Him, we may all gasp in horror and sadness that our officials cannot do more because they don't have enough real authority and power.

So we in Messianic Jewish ministry debate among ourselves. Should we shift all our efforts now to *aliyah?* This would be prudent if danger is indeed looming, however unseen it may currently be. But who will listen? And what about the potential danger for all those living in Israel?

Some say we should spend no more effort on building Messianic congregations in the former Soviet Union. The work is too slow and difficult, and the need is too great. And we hear that ominous warning that Messianic congregations would be easy targets for the anti-Semites. Let all the Jews who remain simply fit into the best churches. Let us teach the pastors to appreciate the call of the Jewish people to return to the land of Israel. Let the Jews become disciples in the churches, because there they could hide out if the times became difficult.

This promise of safety is illusory. None of us have the ability to guarantee the safety of the Jewish people if another incarnation of the Nazis is manifest. Not only that, but none of us can forget the actual history of our people in Europe. There were thousands—perhaps hundreds of thousands—of Jews who had converted to Christianity. Yet baptized Jews were not generally spared the Nazi wrath. They too were humiliated and despised, reduced to ashes by a regime animated by fierce hatred both for Jews and for all people of faith. The Christians in Sudan, in Saudi Arabia, in Armenia, in Uganda, in China, in Russia, Ukraine, Latvia, Estonia, Lithuania, Belarus, and a host of other places already know that they were not spared persecution during the times of trouble.

So do we abandon our efforts to plant new Messianic congregations because of the danger and potential threat? I think not. This is a simple idea to me. Planting new congregations is the outcome of wanting to bring the gospel to people, forming them into disciples. The growth in the number of believers in an area is always accompanied by the growth in the number of congregations. In other words, as congregations grow in number, each with a distinct calling, then the kingdom of God normally grows. New congregation planting is one of the key proven strategies to bring more people into the kingdom of God.

But is it enough simply to plant new Messianic congregations? Will the Messianic movement be able to assume the entire responsibility for the spiritual restoration of the Jewish people? I believe that the work is too great and the calling to colabor too strong for the Messianic Jews to singlehandedly assume this role. In fact, I believe it will be through certain spiritual partnerships and strategic alliances that Jewish evangelism and discipleship are extended. So we who are Messianics must embrace those outside our own movement and find those who are also called to "carry your sons in their arms, and to bring your daughters on their shoulders."

Messianic Jewish sectarianism will fail us. Though it might promise us strength and purity of Jewish identity, it will ultimately be one more false hope. We are part of the body of Messiah, and there are other parts that "sure don't look Jewish" because they *aren't* Jewish. This is the actual nature of Yeshua's kingdom. It includes both Jews and non-Jews. We Jews can't, nor should we, force our Jewishness upon other believers. Neither can we abandon our Jewishness, as if it is insignificant and meaningless. Assimilation into a Gentile culture will not accomplish

God's purposes for the Jews. Even if we have been hidden beneath generations of intermarriage and assimilation, God will yet call for us, calling us by name, and we will hear and will need to respond.

In a way, our Jewishness is like a mine that contains precious stones and metals. It will take digging and then refining in order to obtain all that is valuable. We may have to throw out a lot of dirt and debris. The dross will surely come to the surface, and we must allow it to be skimmed off. Though it had been comingled with us, the dross is neither silver nor gold, and we dare not hold on to it with sentimentality or protectiveness.

What then can we do with confidence? What can we advocate that others do also? I would like to outline an agenda for the future. Before I describe the details, let me say something very important: There are so many things that could be done, but the only unforgivable act is to do nothing of substance. Our only failure will come from doing nothing. As you consider all the things that you *could* do, and develop your own sense of what God's Spirit is *calling you to do,* remember this. Do *something.* Do *anything.* As long as it is born of faith and wisdom, you will be guided, equipped, and redirected as necessary. There are so many worthwhile opportunities. Take any one of them, and God will bless you.

Opportunities for Ministry

1. *Become involved with Messianic congregations.* Visit them. Invite their rabbi and worship team to come to your church. Become a sister congregation to a new Messianic congregation in the former Soviet Union or Israel.

2. *Put off the elder brother's attitude, and put on the Father's heart.*

3. *Purge yourself of anti-Semitism.* Practice not sitting in judgment of the splinters in the eyes of others while ignoring the board in your own eye.

4. *"Do to the least of these, My brothers."*

5. *Overcome with the word of your testimony and the blood of Yeshua.*

6. *Pray for the peace of Jerusalem.*

7. *Share your prosperity.* Be generous in giving to those Jewish people in need and to Messianic Jewish ministries that are making a difference.

8. *Feed Jewish people.* There are thousands of elderly Jews in the former Soviet Union who have such meager pensions that they are on the brink of starvation. You can help by supporting a ministry that is feeding them.

9. *Gather in the lost.* Find those who have lost their Jewish identity and help rebuild it. Encourage intermarried couples to raise their children as Jews. Share the gospel with those who are lost spiritually.

10. *Minister healing.* Jewish people, like all others, have wounds in their souls and diseases in their bodies. Pray for their healing, and watch God's compassion and mercy be released. Make sure you don't simply listen to Jewish *kvetching,* or "complaints," but respond with faithful prayer.

11. *Encourage Jews to be Jewish.* Remind Jews that they have the honor of raising their children as Jews and continuing in the covenant God has

established with the Jewish people.

12. *Provoke to jealousy.* Live a life of faithfulness to the God of Israel in a way that is visible and demonstrates that He is alive. Share the testimony of how you came to love the Jewish Messiah so that Jewish people will want to know Him personally.

13. *Learn about Judaism.* Learn to celebrate and appreciate its rich heritage and traditions, its emphasis on concrete acts of mercy and kindness, and its commitment to community and family.

14. *Find ways to stand with Messianic Jews.* Visit a Messianic congregation. Invite a Messianic leader to speak at your church, in your Sunday school, or at your home group. When Messianic evangelists or missionaries come to your city, attend their events. Find a Messianic ministry that you would like to support with your prayers and finances.

15. *Express appreciation to God for His faithfulness to the Jewish people.* Give Him thanks for preserving a remnant and for His glorious plans to revive and restore the Jewish people. Thank Him that Jewish people gave you your Bible, your Messiah, and introduced the world to the knowledge of God. Ask Him to protect Jerusalem and to prosper the Jewish people.

16. *Find ways to serve the needy Jewish people somewhere in the world.* There may be new Russian-Jewish immigrants in your city who could use your help. There are thousands of

Ethiopian Jews who have moved to Israel who need financial and material help. There are Jews who want to move to Israel but lack money for passports and transportation.

17. *Experiment with celebrating the biblical Jewish holidays.* Join with Messianic congregations in their celebrations. Learn by reading how you can incorporate the rich traditions of the Jewish people into your family heritage.

CLOSING BLESSING

If you have made it to the end, I hope your heart has been either pricked or encouraged. If you were unconcerned or unaware, I hope that has been remedied. If you were already aware of your calling, I hope that you have renewed and clarified your commitment and considered how you can extend your ministry on behalf of the Jewish people.

May God prepare your heart and give you understanding about all that is next.

When God called Abraham, He made a promise that He would bless everyone who blessed Abraham and curse those who cursed him. As you bless the Jewish people, you will receive God's own blessing. While many times we think of blessing as a prayer of thanks—such as a blessing at mealtime—there are two other kinds of blessings. When Jews say a blessing over food, they actually bless God for giving the food. Our prayers typically start with the words, "Blessed are you, O Lord, King of the Universe," and then continue with specifics about the food, be it bread, wine, fruits, or vegetables. It is God whom we are blessing.

There is another kind of blessing, and this is pronounced over people. When the patriarchs blessed their sons, they spoke a blessing that had true prophetic power and anointing. In fact, some blessings are really prophecies, declarations of God's Word to a person about their purpose, character, and destiny. The descendants of Aaron were directed to speak a blessing to the children of Israel. Found in Numbers 6:24–26, this has become known as the Aaronic benediction. As a descendant of Aaron, through the tribe of Levi, I carry on this tradition, and speak this blessing over all who take up the cause of the Jewish people in this hour.

· ·

May the Lord bless you, and keep watch over you.
May the Lord cause the light of His face to shine
brightly upon you, and may He give you favor and grace.
May the Lord lift up His face to you — even smiling upon you
— and give you **shalom,** *peace, through the Prince of Peace,*
Yeshua HaMashiach.
AMEN.

The Bible says that by this blessing God will put His name upon the children of Israel and bless them. As those who bless the sons and daughters of Abraham, may He also put His name upon you and upon your children, and bless you too.

Shalom!

NOTES

CHAPTER ONE

1. Joel Marcus, *Jesus and the Holocaust* (New York: Doubleday, 1997), 46.

CHAPTER FIVE

1. Johannes Hirschmann, S. J., "Schwester Teresia Benedicta vom Heiligen Kreuz", in *Monatsschrift des Budes Neudeutschland,* 34 Jg., 1981, pp. 125–26 as cited in Waltraud Herbstrith, *Edith Stein: A Biography,* San Francisco: Ignatius Press, 1985), English edition, pp. 194–95.

CHAPTER SIX

1. Viktor Frankl, *Man's Search for Meaning* (Boston, MA: Beacon Press, 1992), n.p.

CHAPTER SEVEN

1. Viktor Frankl, *Man's Search for Meaning* (Boston, MA: Beacon Press, 1992), n.p.

GLOSSARY

ADONAI: My Lord.

AHVOT: The fathers. The patriarchs, Abraham, Isaac, and Jacob; the title of the first part of the *Amidah* prayer (see entry below).

ALIYAH: To go up. Jewish immigration to Israel. Used biblically to describe "going up to Jerusalem," which is elevated above all the routes that lead to it.

AMIDAH: Standing. A synonym for the *Shemoneh Esrei* (see entry below), one of the central prayers of the Jewish prayer book, which is prayed while standing.

BABI YAR: A wooded area in Kiev, Ukraine, where tens of thousands of Jews were systematically slaughtered, with their corpses filling the area's ravines. Today a Jewish menorah stands as a memorial to the victims.

BABUSHKA: (*Russian*) grandmother.

BaYOM HaHOO: In That Day. A prophetic term describing the end of this present age.

CHANUKAH: Commemorates the eight days during which the temple was rededicated.

ECCLESSIA: (*Greek*) The called-out ones. Used in the Septuagint (Greek translation of Jewish Scriptures) to translate Hebrew words for "congregation."

ECHAD: One. Used to describe a complex unity. A husband and wife are to become *echad* flesh. The *Shema* declares that God is *echad*.

ESCHATON: (*Greek*) The end of time and the end of the earth.

GALUT: Exile. The *Diaspora,* or scattering, of the Jews outside of the land of Israel.

GERIM: Sojourners; aliens. Those Gentiles who, like Ruth, identify with the Jewish people and their God without converting to Judaism.

GOYIM: Nations. Translated into English as *Gentiles,* this does not describe countries or geopolitical units so much as nationalities or ethnic groups.

HALACHA: Walking. Orthodox Jewish law covering daily application of commandments from *Tanakh* and *Talmud.*

HAOLAM HABAH: The world to come. The realm of eternity.

HAOLAM HAZEH: This world. The realm of this present age.

HORA: Jewish folk dance.

KADDISH: Jewish prayer during mourning.

KIPPAH: Jewish skullcap or yarmulke.

MATZAH: Unleavened bread.

MASHIACH: Anointed one, Messiah.

MIKVAH: Bath for Jewish immersion; antecedent of baptism.

MITZVOT: Commandments.

MOSHE RABBEINU: Moses our Teacher. Term and title of respect for Israel's Lawgiver.

NEVI'IM: Prophets. The prophetic books of the Jewish Scriptures.

NOTZRIM: Modern Hebrew term for Christians.

PIDYON HABEN: Redemption of the firstborn. Ceremony of symbolic redemption of all firstborn Jewish males.

POGROM: *(Russian)* A violent attack or riot against Jews.

SEDER: Home-based celebration of the Feast of Passover.

SHABBAT: The seventh day of creation, and the day of rest.

SHAVUOT: Weeks, or sevens. The Jewish feast commemorating the giving of the *Torah* on Mount Sinai. In Greek, Pentecost, it is also the holiday on which the Holy Spirit was poured out upon the early Messianic Jews.

SHEMA: *Listen, hearken.* The foremost prayer of the Jewish people found in Deuteronomy 6:4, the *Shema* is a call to listen to God and to love Him with all that we are.

SHEMONEH ESREI: *Eighteen.* A central prayer of the Jewish liturgy, it originally had eighteen portions, though a nineteenth was later added. Prayed while standing, it is also called the *Amidah*.

SHEOL: The eternal destination of those who reject God.

SHOFAR: Ram's horn. The distinctive trumpet of the Jewish people, fashioned from a ram's horn, or the horn of other Israeli animals.

SIDDUR: A Jewish prayer book.

SUKKOT: The Feast of Tabernacles.

TANAKH: An acronym for the Jewish Bible formed from the first letters of each of its three parts, *Torah* (first five books of Moses), *Nevi'im* (the Prophets), and *Ketuvim* (the Writings). Called the Old Testament by Christians.

TELOS: *(Greek)* Goal, purpose.

TIKKUN: *Repair.* Acts of mercy and righteousness, which help repair our broken world.

TORAH: Instruction; law. First five Books of Moses.

T'SHUVAH: Return, turn around. Repent, by turning to God, and by turning away from all idolatry and falsehood.

TSURIS: Sorrow, grief.

YOM KIPPUR: Day of Atonement.

YESHUA: Salvation from God. The birth name of Messiah.

RECOMMENDED READING LIST

Brown, Michael. *Our Hands Are Stained With Blood: The Tragic Story of the "Church" and the Jewish People.* Shippensburg, PA: Destiny Image Publisher, 1992. A tough examination of Christian anti-Semitism.

Buber, Martin. *On the Bible: Eighteen Studies.* Ed. Nahum N. Glatzer. New York: Schocken Books, 1968. A fascinating study of the Jewish Scriptures, rich in original insights, by this noted Jewish thinker.

Charlesworth, James H., editor. *Jesus' Jewishness: Exploring the Place of Jesus Within Early Judaism.* Philadelphia, PA: American Interfaith Institute; New York: Crossroad, 1991. An excellent one-volume look at the Jewish identity and character of Jesus.

Dixon, Murray. *The Rebirth and the Restoration of Israel.* Chichester, England: Sovereign Word, 1988. An introduction to modern Israel, this book also documents those who have stood with the Jewish people, such as the Christian Zionists, and those Christians who were anti-Semites.

Donin, Rabbi Hayim Halevy. *To Be a Jew: A Guide to Jewish Observance in Contemporary Life.* New York: Basic Books, 1972. *To Pray as a Jew: A Guide to the Prayer Book and the Synagogue Service.* New York: Basic Books, 1980. Two books that dig deep into a more meaningful Judaism.

Fackenheim, Emil L. *The Jewish Bible After the Holocaust: A Re-reading.* Bloomington, IN: Indiana University Press, 1990. An important Jewish reexamination, asking hard questions in light of Jewish suffering.

Flannery, Edward H. *The Anguish of the Jews: Twenty-Three Centuries of Anti-Semitism.* New York: MacMillan, 1965.

The classic study on anti-Semitism.

Fox, Everett, translator. *The Five Books of Moses: Genesis, Exodus, Leviticus, Deuteronomy, Numbers: A New Translation With Introduction, Commentary, and Notes.* New York: Schocken Books, 1995. An impressive, invigorating translation from the Hebrew, carrying the language's texture and color into English.

Frankl, Viktor E. *Man's Search for Meaning.* Boston: Beacon Press, fourth edition, 1992. A seminal look at the meaningfulness of suffering by a Holocaust survivor.

Gay, Ruth. *Unfinished People: Eastern European Jews Encounter America.* New York: W. W. Norton and Co., 1996.

Herbstrith, Waltraud. *Edith Stein: A Biography.* Trans. Bernard Bonowitz. San Francisco: Harper & Row, 1985. A biography of the Jewish woman, turned Catholic nun, who joined her people in death during the Holocaust.

Heschel, Abraham Joshua. *God in Search of Man: A Philosophy of Judaism.* New York: Meridian Books, 1955. High theological ponderings by a noted Jewish scholar.

Johnson, Paul. A *History of the Jews.* New York: Harper & Row, 1987. A good one-volume historical read.

Kjaer-Hansen, Kai. *Joseph Rabinowitz and the Messianic Movement: The Herzl of Jewish Christianity.* Trans. Birger Petterson. Edinburgh: Handsel Press; Grand Rapids, MI: Wm. B. Eerdsmans, 1995. Choppy, but worth the work.

Kuznetsov, Anatoly, *Babi Yar: A Documentary Novel.* Trans. Zvi Ofer. Jerusalem: Shikmona Publishers in cooperation with Israel Broadcasting Authority, 1983. The now-classic account of the infamous death site in Kiev, Ukraine, where tens of thousands of Jews were slaughtered. Extremely well-written.

Levi, Primo. *The Reawakening.* Trans. Stuart Woolf. New

York: Collier Books, 1986. *If Not Now, When?* Trans. William Weaver. New York: Summit Books, 1985, and other works on the Holocaust. Though his works are translated into English from his native Italian, Levi is a gifted writer. Every word is worth reading.

Losin, Yigal. *Pillar of Fire: The Rebirth of Israel—A Visual History.* Trans. Zvi Ofer. Jerusalem: Shikmona Publishers in cooperation with the Israel Broadcasting Authority, 1983. A pictorial look at the founding of Israel and modern Jewish history.

Marcus, Joel. *Jesus and the Holocaust: Reflections on Sufferings and Hope.* New York: Doubleday, 1997. A provocative and powerful look at the suffering of Jesus and the suffering of the Jews by a Jewish Christian scholar.

Novak, David. *Jewish-Christian Dialogue: A Jewish Justification.* New York: Oxford University Press, 1989. Christians and Jews should talk (though not Messianic Jews, whom he despises), in order to compare notes on what God is saying.

Oestericher, John. *The Unfinished Dialogue: Martin Buber and the Christian Way.* New York: Philosophical Library, 1986.

Prince, Derek. *Prophetic Destinies: Who Is Israel? Who Is the Church?* Orlando, FL: Creation House, 1992. A good introduction to the destiny of Israel and the church.

Pritz, Ray. *Nazarene Jewish Christianity: From the End of the New Testament Period Until Its Disappearance in the Fourth Century.* Jerusalem: Magnes Press, Hebrew University; Lediden. E. J. Brill, 1988. Scholastic, through and through, Pritz draws out clear distinctions between the various Jewish groups that were following Yeshua in the early centuries.

Rappel, Yoel, comp. *Yearning for the Holy Land: Hasidic*

Tales of Israel. Trans. Shmuel Himmelstein. New York: Adama Books, 1986. Splendid ponderings from long ago, by those who anticipated the rebirth of Israel.

Shanks, Herschel, editor. *Christianity and Rabbinic Judaism: A Parallel History of Their Origins and Early Development.* Washington, DC: Biblical Archaeology Society, 1992. A helpful introduction for serious students interested in the parallels and interdependencies of the two faith communities.

Soloveitchik, Rabbi Joseph B. *Halakhic Man.* Trans. Lawrence Kaplan. New York: Jewish Publication Society, 1983. A hearty exhortation by a renowned Orthodox rabbi to live rational, *Torah*-based lives.

Soloveitchik, Rabbi Joseph B. *The Lonely Man of Faith.* New York: Doubleday, 1992. This Jewish scholar articulates the existential crisis of those trying to follow God in a secular, scientific world.

Stern, David. *Jewish New Testament: A Translation of the New Testament That Expresses Its Jewishness.* Clarkesville, MD: Jewish New Testament Publications, 1989. *Jewish New Testament Commentary: A Companion Volume to the Jewish New Testament.* Clarksville, MD: Jewish New Testament Publications, 1992.

Messianic Jewish Manifesto. Gaitherburg, MD: Jewish New Testament Publications, 1988. These three amazing books address many deep issues facing all Messianic Jews.

Van Buren, Paul. *A Theology of the Jewish Christian Reality.* New York: Seabury Press, 1980. Highly respectful, perhaps too much sometimes, of the Christian debt to the Jews and the high value of Christians learning from and about Jews.

Wiesel, Elie. *Souls on Fire: Portraits and Legends of Hasidic Masters.* New York: Summit Books, 1972. Wonder-filled stories of the Hasidic rabbis.

ABOUT THE AUTHOR . . .

DAVID LEVINE has been director of congregational development for Hear O Israel Ministries, based in Jacksonville, Florida, since 1994. Together with his wife, Sandy, Levine oversees the planting and growth of Messianic congregations in the former Soviet Union and the United States. Levine was the leader of Congregation Shema Yisrael in Rochester, New York, for several years prior to joining Hear O Israel Ministries. He is ordained as a Messianic rabbi through the International Alliance of Messianic Congregations and Synagogues. Levine's first career was in broadcast journalism and management. He hosted a radio talk show on family issues in the mid-seventies. He is a conference speaker, seminar leader, and the author of numerous articles and papers on issues touching on Messianic Judaism, the Jewish roots of Christianity, and pastoral philosophy and practice. He was a member of the editorial advisory board for the newly published *Holy Spirit Encounter Bible,* published by Creation House.

Raised in a Conservative Jewish family in Roanoke, Virginia, Levine began following Yeshua (Jesus) in 1976. He is married to Sandy Levine and has two children, Chris Vaughan and Allison D'Aurizio.

SANDY LEVINE is David's partner in ministry and is actively involved with him in all phases of ministry. Though not Jewish, Sandy has served as president of a local Hadassah chapter, a Jewish women's Zionist organization. Sandy has been an entrepreneur, starting an indoor plant and gift store and a specialty food company. She is a conference speaker, women's retreat organizer, and author of a series of poems on the modern state of Israel. Sandy and David are members of the board of directors of Christian Alliance for Israel, an organization dedicated to building Christian understanding and support for the Jewish people and Israel.